Linking Literacy and

Popular Culture:

Finding Connections

for Lifelong Learning

Linking Literacy and Popular Culture:

Finding Connections

for Lifelong Learning

Ernest Morrell

Christopher-Gordon Publishers, Inc.
Norwood, Massachusetts

Credits

Christopher-Gordon Publishers, Inc.
1502 Providence Highway, Suite #12
Norwood, Massachusetts 02062
800-934-8322
781-762-5577

Printed in the United State of America
10 9 8 7 6 5 4 3 2 1   07 06 05 04

ISBN: 1-929024-70-3
Library of Congress Catalogue: 2003114100

To the students at

North and South Bay High Schools

and to mom and dad, my first teachers.

Contents

Part Two: The Practice

Acknowledgments

I would like to thank Pedro Noguera, Jabari Mahiri, Glynda Hull, Anne Haas Dyson, and the late John Ogbu, members of the faculty at the University of California at Berkeley, for their guidance, inspiration, and advice during the early portion of this work. I would also like to acknowledge my two closest friends and colleagues, Jeff Duncan-Andrade and Wayne Yang, for the countless conversations about the relationship between popular culture and secondary teaching. The late-night conversations with the two of you were my most valuable learning experiences.

I would like to issue special thanks Jeannie Oakes and John Rogers, directors of the Institute for Democracy, Education, and Access (IDEA) at the University of California at Los Angeles for their support, financial and personal, of my work with the students at South Bay High school. I would also like to thank Sue Canavan, of Christopher-Gordon Publishers, for her faith in this project and her enduring support over the two years that it took to complete this manuscript. Thanks Sue, for the patience that allowed me to find and arrange these many words.

And, finally, I would like to thank the students of North and South Bay High Schools who continually inspired me to become a teacher and person worthy of their faith and trust in me. This book, more than anything, is a tribute to you.

Preface

My mother, who has been a teacher for over 30 years, claims to have seen more reforms than she can count. "What's next?" She muses during a familiar Christmas conversation of educators. Yet she and my father, who has also been a teacher for over 30 years, continue to search for answers. At a local bookstore they peruse the meager education section for new titles even though both are within two years of retirement.

During department meetings at the high school where I taught, veteran teachers would claim that the students were changing. They were right; the pupils who now sat in their classrooms spoke different languages, lived in different communities, and faced different realities than those who sat in the same desks a generation earlier. If this is the case, then how can the same lessons reach them?

My students throughout the years have claimed that most of the adults in their lives do not understand them. They are also right. Often removed by age and circumstances, even the best instruction, filled with care and good intentions, is lost in translation.

This book is written for my parents and the other veterans who live to teach. It is written for the myriad of students I have met who thirst to learn. I have not attempted to offer yet another reform nor have I attempted to denigrate the teachers and students I have come to respect and love.

I have written a book to honor the rapidly changing world while also honoring the seemingly timeless goals of educators; to teach the tools of social and cultural significance to another generation; to create good workers and, more importantly, to inspire good citizens. I believe that linking popular culture to academic literacy instruction will enable teachers and students to co-create connections between the ever evolving world and the worlds of words and ideas. I hope that what I have written aids somewhat in this process.

Ernest Morrell

Part One
The Prospect

Chapter 1

Introduction

The Challenge and Opportunity Facing Literacy Educators in 21st Century Classrooms

Being a teacher of language and literacy is hard enough these days, as if it were ever easy. Literacy educators in today's K-12 classrooms are particularly challenged, given their tremendous responsibilities under increasingly difficult circumstances. At no time in the history of American education has the development of academic literacy skills been so important to the social and economic well-being of all citizens (Alvermann, 2001). Only a generation ago, students who did not perform well in school could obtain well-paying jobs in manufacturing or the trades that would enable them to live comfortable and fulfilled lives. The loss of America's industrial base to technological advances and the outsourcing of manufacturing jobs to developing nations have left a two-tiered employment structure; one tier features increases in technical employment and high-paying jobs for those able to secure the necessary skills to perform them. On the other end of the employment spectrum are service industry jobs that pay barely livable wages. These jobs too are abundant, if undesirable. The bottom line for today's students is that in order to contend for the American Dream, students need to develop a high level of literacy in school, placing increasing pressure on literacy educators to help them acquire those skills. The alleged literacy crisis in today's schools is not so much a testament to regressing classroom instruction and student achievement as it is a testament to the increasing literacy demands of a postindustrial, techno-literate society.

3

Literacy educators are also challenged by the overwhelming social, linguistic, cultural, and economic diversity in America's classrooms, particularly those classrooms located within or near metropolitan areas. I know that categorizing diversity as a challenge rather than a strength is problematic, but bear with me. I say that the growing diversity is a challenge because, while students are bringing into our classrooms an array of experiences that can and should enrich literacy-learning environments, they also bring different background experiences with literacy, different language practices, and different learning styles. Too often, what happens in literacy classrooms is that the students whose experiences, practices, and preferences most closely resemble the demands of academic literacy are rewarded, while those whose experiences, practices, and preferences are less congruent, struggle with the development of academic literacy (Gee, 1996).

What can happen, what needs to happen, is that teachers create environments in which students can learn from each other's diverse language and literacy experiences how to see the world differently and how to participate more fully as critical citizens in a multicultural democracy. This ability to understand the various purposes and functions of language and literacy in society I associate with the term *critical literacy*. The ability to use language and literacy to participate fully as a citizen I call *civic literacy*. I will speak more about critical and civic literacies throughout the book. For the present, however, it is important to consider that the mission of literacy education has to be broader than the development of academic or professional literacies. Further, the various language and literacy practices that seem to offer a challenge, when thinking about the development of academic and professional literacies, are a tremendous resource for helping students to develop critical and civic literacies. Of course, I am going to make the case that students' background knowledge can assist with the learning of academic literacy as well, but that comes later. There has to be some reason to read the book.

Given all that I've said, it becomes evident why finding effective ways to develop academic and critical literacies among students across multiple lines of difference is perhaps the greatest imperative in education today. As I've mentioned, there are serious social, cultural, and economic consequences associated with the acquisition of academic literacy skills. In addition to the positive correlations that I have mentioned between literacy development, professional employment, and economic empowerment, there are also negative social and economic outcomes for those students who are not able to acquire these literacies in school. There is, for instance, an inverse correlation between academic literacy development and prison incarceration rates for African-American males, who, though they only comprise 6% of the nation's population, comprise nearly one-half of the prison population. Studies have revealed that the overwhelming majority of these men lack the basic academic literacy skills to integrate into society. There are also connections between academic illiteracy and teen pregnancies for young women. Literally, for poor and disenfranchised students, acquiring these literacies of power is a matter of life and death. The only social institutions equipped to help young women and men acquire these skills are America's schools, which means high stakes for those who undertake the responsibility of becoming literacy educators. It is not a job to be entered into lightly, yet it is not a task without its rewards.

I've already alluded to this, but I want to talk in more detail about the changing face of America's classrooms, frequently referred to as the *demographic imperative*. That is, public school students are becoming increasingly diverse with respect to culture, ethnicity, primary language, and socioeconomic status, while the diversity among the pool of prospective teachers diminishes. For instance, the *Digest of Education Statistics* (1998) forecasts that, in the next decade, the percentage of ethnic minority teachers will shrink to 5%, while the enrollment of ethnic minority children in America's schools will grow to 41%.

A generation of teachers are being sent to increasingly diverse environments to teach students who do not look like them and do not share similar upbringing experiences, life chances, or world outlook (Foster, 1998; Hudson and Holmes, 1994; Hunter-Boykin, 1992). The resulting uncertainty, mistrust, miscommunication, and academic underachievement have also had a tremendous impact on the teaching population, contributing to low morale and high attrition, a walking exodus from the classrooms of America, a revolving door from the teacher education programs through classrooms and back out into law schools, Ph.D. programs, or corporate offices in a span as short as three to five years (Darling-Hammond, 2000). This real, yet unfortunate, process leaves children, their parents (especially the low-income ones), and the greater society truly left in the blur, wondering what went wrong and what to do differently.

These challenging classrooms, however, are also the perfect site for struggle for those literacy educators who are dedicated to the cause of social justice and want to be major players in helping those students who have traditionally not had access to the literacy skills needed for advancement and empowerment in our society. Even though this is a time of tremendous challenge, it should also be viewed as a time of tremendous opportunity for those critical educators who see teaching as a revolutionary and political act. Teachers, as informed cultural workers, can create the conditions whereby all students can develop the necessary tools for enacting critical citizenship and obtaining competitive employment in a techno-cultural, post-modern global economy. These teachers are key architects in the creation of sensitive and informed citizens who are able to contribute economically, socially, culturally, and politically to a new global republic. In short, these are teachers who change the world (Oakes and Lipton, 1999).

I am certain that the questions are already swirling; the questions that challenge us daily as literacy educators. How is this to be done? How can we develop and implement a critical agenda when our students need the academic literacy skills for all of the reasons provided in the opening paragraphs? How can we create cohesive classroom communities and develop sensitive, yet challenging and enriching, curricula that meet the needs of all of our students, given that their respective needs are so varied? I didn't say it would be easy, but I do believe it is possible. And *my* answer (as opposed to *the* answer) will take a little longer than a paragraph to explain. Essentially, my response to these questions that have plagued me throughout my career is this book, which I now share with you.

A first important step in this transformative process for literacy educators is learning to see all students as learners and users of language and literacy before they enter the classroom. Too often, many students are viewed as deficits that hold no relevant knowledge to be drawn upon by their teachers to improve scholastic achievement (Ladson-Billings, 1994). To the contrary, this book encourages teachers to examine the everyday language and literacy practices of their students that are associated with membership in particular cultures and communities. I advocate that teachers become ethnographers of the language and literacy practices in the neighborhoods and homes of their students. I will speak more about what I mean by ethnographies of literacy throughout the book, but

I am attracted to ethnography as a form of teacher research because ethnographic investigations, when performed correctly, are inherently additive rather than deficit oriented. That is, ethnographies, rather than attempting to understand how other cultures are different from and less than our own, set out to learn how different cultures make sense of the world on their own terms, which implies a logic and purpose to all linguistic and cultural practices (Geertz, 2000).

Through the course of my career as a teacher and researcher, I have had the opportunity to participate in several of these ethnographies of literacy. As a result, I have come to understand that many youth who experience difficulty in school, have valuable literacy skills that they have developed through their participation in youth and popular culture (Morrell, 2002). I argue in this book that, by building upon students' literacy experiences with popular culture in non-school settings, teachers can make authentic and powerful connections between students' worlds and the demands of the classroom.

I want to state emphatically from the beginning that something can be done in the face of all of these challenges to increase the literacy skills of the myriad youth who are failing in America's schools. Though I begin with an explicit acknowledgment of the challenges and obstacles that confront students and teachers in literacy classrooms, I have written what I feel is an optimistic book; a practical book that is filled with tangible examples and reasons for hope. So don't put it away or write it off as another cynical denigration of the content and quality of secondary literacy instruction. Far to the contrary, it is a rallying call for a revolutionary practice that can deliver results in literacy classrooms. Some of the sections may seem dense or esoteric (such as the discussion of cultural theory), or just foreign (such as cultural anthropology and ethnography), but it is all important to developing the knowledge base that teachers need to become practitioners that make innovative use of popular culture as well as the researchers and textual producers who play the leading roles in redefining the nature of the discipline.

This text draws upon several years of practitioner-research I conducted in urban secondary English classrooms, where I used popular culture to make connections between the local literacy practices of my adolescent students and the academic, professional, critical, and civic literacies required for success in school and society. In this book I provide a comprehensive, theoretically grounded, and empirically tested approach to teaching popular culture in schools that promotes academic and critical literacy development among these youth. The book is intended for those preservice teachers and novices just learning how to teach, for veteran teachers, and for teacher educators who, given the current demographic shifts among the teaching and student populations, are increasingly challenged to find ways to authentically connect with diverse students in American schools.

I begin this voyage, necessarily, by reflecting upon my own cultural history, specifically as it relates to my involvement with popular culture as an adolescent. These seminal experiences with popular culture have affected my outlook and output as a teacher and researcher. I next briefly outline several important theoretical concepts and terms essential to an informed discussion of this topic that emanate from literacy and cultural theories, some of which I have already begun to use. I follow the theoretical introduction by introducing the two schools, North Bay High and South Bay High, where I conducted this research. Finally, I offer a brief overview of the remaining chapters in the book.

I was born in the city where North Bay High School is located and spent my early years in an urban neighborhood of the city. My father was a minister in this same neighborhood for 17 years, and my mother taught pre-school and kindergarten there for over 25 years. My grandmother, aunts, uncles, and numerous cousins also live in this city and, for most of the 6 years that I taught in the district, I lived within a mile of the high school. I say this because I had a vested interest in the success of North Bay's students and an intimate knowledge of and involvement with the community and school site.

As an African-American youth growing up in a metropolitan area during the 1970s and 1980s, I was very much a participant in the emergent youth popular culture, which played a dominant role in my identity development as it did with many of my counterparts. From junior high school through college, my world revolved around popular culture, particularly music and film. This included my haircut, my dress, my language, and, of course, my walk. It was through popular culture that I first became politicized watching Spike Lee's *Do The Right Thing* and listening to Public Enemy's "Fight the Power" during my senior year of high school. I was also known to wear an assortment of Africa medallions in honor of the motherland and the struggle to free Nelson Mandela and the black South

Africans from the oppression of Apartheid. This, too, was a part of the popular culture, inserting its way into clothes, songs, billboards, and popular language. That summer, after high school graduation, I read Alex Haley's *Roots* in its entirety. This was one of the first books that I ever read cover to cover and it was largely attributable to my inspiration from the Spike Lee film that I repeatedly watched and referenced via the accompanying hip-hop soundtrack during that summer. The feature song on that album, entitled "Fight the Power," urged young citizens to question and, more importantly, to resist. It was through this album that I first began to reflect on my educational experience, questioning which texts I had been forced to read, who had been portrayed as heroic, what values had been promoted, and who had been left out. That summer, I made a list of all of the important people and events that were alluded to in the song and in the album that had been absent from my elementary and secondary curricula and I made it my goal to learn about them on my own. This led to my reading Haley's book, positioning myself as a critical intellectual, and making a series of personal choices that ultimately led me into urban schools and classrooms as an educator committed to social change. This critical involvement with popular culture would continue through college and into adulthood. As I was learning how to position myself as an activist and an intellectual, I was also becoming aware that popular culture was the lens through which I would view and make sense of the world.

I feel it important to state up front that I do not come to this task as a blank slate on the subject of popular culture and its impact on youth. I believe that I was profoundly and positively impacted by my engagement with elements of popular culture such as popular film and hip-hop as an urban youth of color, and my experiences, certainly provide a counterbalance to the mostly negative attention that popular culture and its youth participants receive from mainstream educators and the media. I also realize, though, that as a reflexive researcher (Bourdieu and Wacquant, 1992) I must be sensitive to my own sensitivities and also critical of the role that my positionality plays in simultaneously elucidating and complicating the argument that I am trying to make. I am not seeking to be a proponent of popular culture for the sake of entertainment and uncritical consumption for that would not be helpful to the teachers or the students they seek to help. Rather, my aim is to understand the academic potential of popular culture as well as its relevance to, and resonance with, the lives of America's youth from the standpoint of a critical educator seeking to involve these youth in innovative and revolutionary practices that lead to social, academic, and critical transformations.

Though I am hesitant to preempt this discussion with a multitude of qualifiers and caveats, it is important to make a few disclaimers in an effort to prevent, where possible, the misuse of the material presented within these pages. *Literacy and Popular Culture: Finding Connections for Lifelong Learning* is not intended to provide easy answers to complex problems, nor are its units and activities to be used as cookie-cutter models for fixing the ills of secondary literacy instruction. Please do not copy the sample unit plans from the appendices and hand them in to principals or methods instructors who are demanding such materials. By the time this book reaches you, the popular cultural pieces used for these lessons may already be dated and your students may not even recognize or find interesting the songs and films that were all the rage just a few short years ago. Popular culture changes over time and varies from region to region. There is even variance within communities and schools.

That being said, this book has a great deal to offer secondary literacy educators. It models a process for learning from and with students that is situated in the literacy practices accompanying participation in everyday activity (Cole, 1996). It challenges prevailing wisdom about who owns relevant classroom knowledge and encourages secondary English teachers to learn from their students how to best incorporate popular culture into traditional curricula. Finally, through this book, I have endeavored to paint portraits of classrooms that are fun, engaging, and culturally affirming even as they prepare students for the academic, social, professional, and political demands of their future.

I also want to add that, although my experiences have been primarily in urban settings with impoverished students of color, the lessons shared in this book are relevant to multiple contexts. I believe that all of today's adolescents are participants in popular culture, regardless of race, ethnicity, socioeconomic status, gender, or geography. Indeed, it is the advancement of technology that has allowed popular media to infiltrate every nook and cranny of our existence, creating a global youth culture that transcends these usually divisive categories. One needs only examine the data that analyze popular culture consumption to understand that this is anything but an urban phenomenon. The leading consumers of popular media in the United States (including genres such as hip-hop music, which is generally associated with urban youth) are suburban teens that generally possess superior purchasing power to their urban counterparts.

Popular Culture in Theory and Practice

I now turn from my personal story to my practice as a researcher. Throughout the book, I will be referring to a series of studies that I conducted at two urban high schools over an eight-year period that demonstrate the impact that popular culture can have on literacy development. I am, at the same time, making a larger argument about the importance of classroom teachers functioning as researchers and knowledge producers within the discipline. To service both of these ends, I will speak at length about the decisions I made as a researcher, the theories and concepts I draw upon, the salient terms I set out to define, and the methods I used to analyze the data that I collected during these projects.

As my goal as a practitioner-researcher was to determine the impact of the critical study of popular culture on the development of academic and critical literacy, I focused my unit planning and data analysis on Shirley Bryce Heath's (1983) concept of a *literacy event*. Heath defines a literacy event as, "a communication act that represents any occasion in which a piece of writing is integral to the nature of participants' interactions and their interpretive processes." In subsequent years, several theorists (Ferdman, 1990; Gee, 1996; Mahiri, 1998; Street, 1985) as well as the National Council of Teachers of English (NCTE) (1996) have argued for a broader definition of literacy that includes relevance to culture and technological advances. Keeping Heath's concept of a literacy event, however, I would like to expand the definition to include: *a communicative act in which any text is integral to the nature of participants' interactions and interpretive processes.* According to this expanded definition, both popular films and popular music would be considered as text.

To help with my planning and analysis, I examined literacy theory, critical theory, cultural theory, social theory, and state and federal frameworks for English and Language Arts in an attempt to gain an understanding of academic and critical literacy. Academic literacy, then, refers to those forms of engaging, producing, and dialoging about texts that have value in primary, secondary, and postsecondary education (Harris and Hodges, 1995; Street, 1995;

Venezky et al., 1990). It is important to note, however, that changing technologies and the onset of new (computer, cyber, digital, technical, and video/visual) literacies are transforming notions of what it means to be academically literate (Cushman, Kingten, Kroll, and Rose, 2001). Also, critical literacy theorists explicitly critique academic literacy as privileging some groups while marginalizing others.

Critical literacy is defined as the ability to not only read and write, but to assess texts in order to understand the relationships between power and domination that underlie and inform them (Hull, 1993). Critical literacy can also illuminate the power relationships in society and teach those who are critically literate to participate in and use literacy to change dominant power structures to liberate those who are oppressed by them (Freire and Macedo, 1987). Those who are critically literate are able to understand the socially constructed meaning embedded in texts as well as the political and economic contexts in which texts are embedded. Ultimately, critical literacy can lead to an emancipated worldview and even transformational social action (Freire, 1970; Hull, 1993; McLaren, 1994; UNESCO, 1975).

When I was making sense of the data that I collected from the classroom units, I looked for examples of students debating, critiquing, clarifying, problematizing, and politicizing popular cultural and academic texts. I also looked for examples of students taking ownership of and using the academic language of critique and analysis for their own subversive purposes throughout the research. I decided to focus on literacy events that featured students bridging popular cultural texts and academic texts or concepts, discussing canonical or academic texts or concepts, relating popular cultural texts to their everyday lives, and utilizing the canonical or academic texts or concepts to analyze everyday issues.

My work as a teacher and researcher has been heavily influenced by the new literacy studies. New literacy theorists believe that students are not illiterate per se, as much as they possess literacies that have little connection with the dominant literacies that are promoted through institutions such as public schools (New London Group, 1996; Street, 1995). Often, the failure of students to develop "academic" literacy skills stems not from a lack of intelligence, but from the inaccessibility of the school curriculum to students who do not adhere to the "dominant" or "mainstream" culture. Educators of 21st-century schools, they argue, need to examine the non-school literacy lives of marginalized and disenfranchised youth to find connections between these local literacies and the literacies of schooling. Mahiri (1998), for example, found strong connections between urban youth's literacy practices around participation in popular culture and the types of literacies required in schools or academic literacies. It was in the spirit of the new literacy theorists that I began my work with the students at North and South Bay High Schools, which I will now introduce.

A Tale of Two Schools

North Bay High is an urban, multicultural school of nearly 2200 students located in a large northern California city. The ethnic breakdown of the campus is approximately 40–45% Asian/Asian American (Chinese, Vietnamese, and Southeast Asian), 35% African American, 15% Chicano/Latino, and 5–10% other immigrant groups (i.e., Bosnian, African). There is a less than 1% white American population. At North Bay High, standardized test scores lag far behind state and national norms, the school regularly scores in the twentieth and thirtieth percentile on major standard assessments such as the Stanford 9, the CAP, and CLAS assessments. The median SAT score hovers below 800, which would place an individual student in the tenth percentile nationally. During the years that I taught at this school, 57.9% of the school population was eligible to receive Aid to Families with Dependent Children (AFDC) and only one classroom was wired into the Internet.

My students at North Bay High were much maligned from the staff room to the local news media as violent, unmotivated, and incapable of serious scholarship. "Difficult" literary works gathered dust in the book room adjacent to the library as many of my colleagues surmised that these students simply were not prepared for rigorous literary study. During my first year teaching at North Bay, for instance, a colleague laughed out loud as I explained that I was teaching *Native Son* to my students. "You'll learn," was the knowing retort. On another occasion, the bookroom clerk explained to me that the reason *The Odyssey* texts where seven years older than I was and falling apart was because no one dared to teach such a complicated book. During the 1960s, when the book was ordered, North Bay High was a far more affluent school and the surrounding neighborhoods contained mostly middle-class students. You'll see in later chapters just what my students were able to accomplish with these supposedly inappropriate texts. As a result of these pervasive attitudes, however, students frequently arrived in my classes never having read a complete novel or play and many had little experience with analytical essay writing even though they were nearing the end of their secondary careers.

My most significant challenge, however, was that the students initially embraced these negative images of themselves as illiterate and non-intellectual. Many of them were simply prepared to give up on themselves and their futures. The lack of academic self-esteem was truly heart breaking, particularly given that I could see so much unrealized potential in students who did not see much in themselves. It was my desire as a literacy educator to help students realize their academic potential, while proving society and my colleagues wrong, that ultimately led to the experiences with popular culture that this book reports.

South Bay High School, by comparison, is a diverse multicultural school in a medium-sized southern California city that served both affluent and working-class students. Nestled along southern California's Pacific coast, South Bay is a comprehensive high school with an enrollment of 3100 students. Hailed as a school with a population that closely reflects the demographics of the state of California, South Bay has the following ethnic breakdown: 46.9% white, 32.6% Hispanic, 12.7% African American, and 6.9% Asian. Four hundred and fifteen of the students are listed as English Learners with the overwhelming majority of those being Spanish speakers. Of the graduates, 67.8% are eligible for admission to the state's public universities as opposed to the 36.6% statewide average. A significant percentage of the students, nearly 25%, also qualify to receive free or reduced meals. Sixty-six percent of the teachers at South Bay are white, 17% are Hispanic, 8% African American, and 6% Asian. The average Scholastic Aptitude (SAT) score for South Bay High is 1048 compared to a state average of 1011 and a national average of 1016.

Although these numbers seem to reflect that South Bay High is a successful, or at least above-average, school by traditional criteria, there exist huge disparities in achievement between students according to ethnic and socioeconomic background. The disparities are so great that South Bay High School is often referred to as two schools, one highly successful campus that services the affluent population (which is largely composed of white and Asian-American students who are residents of the northern portion of the city) and another less successful urban school that services the low-income (African American and Latino) students who live either in the Rivera corridor, the poorest section of the city, or commute on permit from nearby cities.

The students that I worked with at South Bay High were members of the second school as low-income students of color who resided either in or near the Rivera corridor, a largely low-income neighborhood of the city, or commuted to campus from impoverished and working-class neighborhoods throughout the greater Los Angeles area. These students were involved in a collaborative project between researchers and graduate students at a nearby university and educators at South Bay High to examine and transform the pathways students of color follow from the beginning of high school into their futures as citizens, community members, and workers. Towards these ends, the intervention/study was originally built around a 9th grade humanities class at South Bay High. Students in the South Bay Project (SBP) became both researchers and research subjects over the course of their four-year involvement, participating in two major summer research seminars held at the university (which I ended up directing) as well as carrying out several research projects as part of their coursework in the project classes at school.

Of the 30 students in the South Bay Project, 29 graduated high school and 25 gained acceptance to four-year universities. By Fall 2001, 16 had enrolled in four-year universities, nine enrolled in two-year colleges, two enrolled in technical schools, one entered the workplace, and one joined the military. These rates of high school graduation, college acceptances, and college attendance rates for minority students are significantly higher than similar students at South Bay High School, as well as in California and in the nation (National Center for Educational Statistics, 1998b).

During my two and a half year involvement with the SBP, I helped to co-teach the project classes and coordinated the summer research seminars, which were offered at a nearby university, while also working as a researcher. In both the classes and the seminars, we used students' experiences and interests as the driving catalyst of the inquiry-based curriculum. We wanted students to develop a language of analysis that enabled them to make sense of an unfair, yet mutable world. We also wanted students to have a sense of empowerment over their own narratives and their own futures. Over the duration of the project, for example, youth participation in hip-hop culture and the portrayal of youth in the media became important topics of study for these students.

Being a teacher, I was very much a participant in the both settings. I do not say this apologetically, for I will argue in many places throughout this book that classroom teachers are uniquely positioned to engage in action research projects that can shed light on many of the difficult issues that we face in the profession. There were, however, occasions for which I needed to distance myself from the action of the classroom, which I attempted to do through the extensive use of audio and video equipment. I also took extensive notes when I could, which usually happened after class. A favorite activity of mine was to watch videotapes of classroom practice and take notes from the video. The data sources I generated include: field notes; video and audio tapes of students working in groups, participating in classroom discussions, and making presentations; transcriptions of conversations and interviews; and examples of student work, including notes, essays, and examinations.

Although wearing two hats in the classroom was sometimes difficult, I believe that this study provides a powerful example of how educators can position themselves as ethnographers of students' cultures and researchers of the practices in their own classrooms. I also believe that the benefits of being intimately related to the students and working with them closely on a daily basis outweighs the drawbacks of attempting to maintain distance and a false sense of objectivity (Cochran-Smith and Lytle, 1993; Kincheloe and McLaren, 1998).

Indeed, a secondary focus of this book is to advocate for more teacher action research—that is research conducted by teachers on their own classroom practice to be shared with pre-service and veteran teachers as well as teacher educators, educational researchers, and educational policy makers. We live and work in an age that is witnessing the deskilling of the craft of teaching (Giroux, 1988) where administrators and policy makers are investing large sums of money into the creation of teacher-proof curricula. During these perilous times for the profession, it is imperative that teachers continue to exert control over the knowledge production associated with their craft and engage in action research projects that investigate and demonstrate innovative and radical classroom practices.

Not only is this important for teachers as individuals and members of a profession, but the production and distribution of action research projects are ultimately important for students, for communities, and for society at large. We have known for some time that critical reflection is important to growth and development as a teacher (Freire, 1997), but it is also important for teachers to share those reflections with others in the profession, whether it is through a book, an article in a practitioner-oriented journal, a conference presentation, or a department-level faculty meeting. This type of sharing, I argue, leads to increased ownership over the profession; but I argue that it will also yield the types of revolutionary practices that will help educators to create dynamic literacy-learning classrooms.

Outline of the Book

This book is divided into three sections: *The Prospect*, *The Practice*, and *The Possibilities*. Chapter 2 taps into critical and cultural theory to provide a grounded, yet accessible definition of popular culture for teachers and teacher educators. Williams (1995) suggests that culture is one of the most complex terms in the English language. He articulates three components of culture that are essential to any thorough analysis of the subject. The first of these components is the *ideal*, in which culture is a state or process of human perfection in terms of absolute or universal values. According to the *documentary* component, culture is the body of intellectual and imaginative work, in which human thought and experience are recorded. Finally, the third, or *social*, component of culture is a description of a particular way of life, which expresses certain meanings and values not only in art and learning, but also in institutions and "ordinary" behavior. The brief definition of popular culture provided in this chapter is inspired by cultural theorists (Docker, 1994; Hall, 1998; McCarthy, 1998; Storey, 1998) who were themselves inspired by Williams along with critical theorists (Adorno and Horkheimer, 1999) and sociologists (Gramsci, 1971). These theorists see popular culture as a site of struggle between the forces of resistance of subordinate groups in society and the forces of incorporation of dominant groups in society. Popular culture, they argue, is neither an imposed mass culture nor a people's culture; it is more of a terrain of exchange between the two. Those who look at popular culture from this perspective tend to see it as a terrain of ideological struggle between dominant and subordinate classes, or dominant and subordinate cultures, expressed through music, film, mass media artifacts, language, customs and values. This definition may differ from "popular" ideas of popular culture as simply songs, movies, and television shows. I argue that there are important differences between "popular" definitions of popular culture and the historical-theoretical definitions I provide in this chapter for teachers interested in using popular culture in their classrooms.

Chapter 3 articulates a rationale for why literacy educators should consider teaching popular culture in their classrooms to promote academic achievement and critical consciousness among their students. This comprehensive annotated list covers a wide range of possible social, cultural, and intellectual impacts for individual students, teachers, and the classroom community as a whole. My desire for this chapter is twofold. One goal is to help educators develop their own rationale for teaching with popular culture by sharing my own. A second goal is to provide educators with a language that enables them to communicate with other important participants in the educational drama who may be somewhat skeptical about the inclusion of popular culture into traditional classroom curricula. Let's be honest, it looks better if it is coming out of a book, right?

The Practice, which is comprised of chapters 4 through 7, analyzes classroom practices to illustrate how the critical teaching of popular culture can produce powerful academic and social outcomes with urban youth. I draw upon classroom data from a series of action research projects conducted during the eight years that I taught urban teens at North and South Bay High Schools. I also include data from observations of secondary English classrooms in my role as a teacher educator in addition to vignettes drawn from a methods course I teach at a major university. Finally, I include a few vignettes from my work with student athletes at a major university who were also having difficulty acquiring literacies of power. I combine the vignettes from the Athletic Study Center at West Coast University with my own experiences as a high school coach to make the case that teachers and coaches can utilize student interest and participation in sports to develop much needed literacy skills. Chapters 4 through 7 each focus on a particular manifestation of popular culture (i.e., music, film, television and media, and sports). In each of these chapters, I begin with actual vignettes from practice, introduce each manifestation of popular culture and explain its significance to the lives of youth. The bulk of each chapter describes and analyzes classroom practices that attempt to incorporate this element of popular culture and discuss possibilities for other literacy educators interested in incorporating popular culture.

Chapter 4 lays out the history and background of hip-hop music and culture, explaining its origins in urban, post-industrial America. It also explains how hip-hop music has grown as a counter-cultural voice of resistance even as it has become co-opted by mainstream, corporate interests. The heart of the chapter, however, presents and analyzes a unit I taught that used hip-hop as a bridge to canonical poetry. I explain the rationale for the unit, the various goals and objectives, the class activities, and share classroom experiences, samples of student dialogue and student work, and excerpts from interviews I conducted with students at the unit's conclusion. In this chapter I also describe a project in which a team of high school students from the South Bay Project investigate the impact of hip-hop culture on youth in America along with its potential uses in high school classrooms. I describe the project, its context as part of a larger seminar on youth research, and present examples of the students involved in research along with excerpts from their final presentation and report.

Chapter 5 focuses on the critical teaching of popular film texts in secondary English classrooms. After outlining the rationale for shifting the focus of the English classroom to include critical film studies, I highlight two classroom units that incorporated popular film into the traditional curriculum. The first unit began with *The Godfather* trilogy and incorporated Homer's *The Odyssey*. Another unit joined Richard Wright's *Native Son* with the John Grisham novel-based film *A Time to Kill*. In creating and evaluating the units, I started with three basic goals: to analyze the viability of utilizing popular culture to develop critical and analytical skills; to assess the potential for providing students with activities and techniques that would facilitate a transfer of these skills from popular cultural texts into/onto the literary and academic texts from the canon; and to determine the capacity of this approach to enable students to critique the messages sent to them through the literary canon as well as the societal institutions that permeated their lives, such as the popular cultural media and urban schools.

To evaluate the class's progress towards these goals, I analyzed classroom discourse and student written work for examples of engagements with literary texts that demonstrated mastery and social critique. From my analysis, I found that students were not only able to thoroughly engage *The Odyssey* and *Native Son*, but they were also able to apply Wright's critique of racism and injustice to their own situation attending an urban high school. The students ultimately decided to fight back by contacting the local media and creating a magazine, entitled *Serious Voices of Urban Youth,* that shed light on the injustices and inequities that students faced at their high school.

Chapter 6 looks at ways that teachers can promote critical analyses of the mainstream media. In this chapter I share and analyze data gathered during a summer program I coordinated in which urban teens learned to become critical researchers studying urban youth's access to public spaces and social institutions. One research team decided to study urban youth's access to the corporate media and the corporate media's portrayal of urban youth. To attack their research question, these students read relevant literature relating to critical media literacy and the sociology of education, designed a study, conducted interviews, analyzed countless hours of news coverage, and performed a content analysis of major daily newspapers from across the nation. This chapter follows these teens through their research process, looking at the implications of this process for their literacy development and literacy education.

Chapter 7 highlights a program that two high school coaches (myself and a colleague), who were also English teachers, used to make connections between sports and academic literacy for the members of their girls' basketball team. This chapter surveys existing research that has highlighted the literacy practices associated with participation in sports and presents the rationale and the structure of the basketball program as it relates to literacy development. The chapter contains several vignettes showing how participation in a basketball program was used to develop academic reading and writing. It also discusses the impact of the program on the girls' ability to develop empowering literacies—new ways of reading themselves and their world. Nearly all of the student-athletes who completed the program attended four-year universities, many among the most elite universities in the nation. Several also became extremely active in promoting critical literacy within their local community.

I also report data from my experiences with the Athletic Study Center at a major university. At West Coast University, I worked with student athletes who were in jeopardy of being expelled from school. In my work, I was able to utilize the athletes' experience and expertise gained from involvement in sports to help them learn the skills needed to succeed in the classroom. The young men who participated in the center's study skills program were also able to increase academic reading and writing while learning to see themselves and society differently.

Chapter 8 speaks to the countless teachers who are excited about the possibilities of teaching popular culture, yet feel unprepared to do so. The chapter points to the importance of educators seeking alternatives to the traditional methods of engaging students and offers, as an alternative, a critical pedagogy (Freire, 1970; Giroux, 1997; hooks, 1994; McLaren, 1994) in which students and teachers learn from each other while engaging in authentic dialogue that is centered in the experiences of urban youth. It also speaks to the importance of teachers creating classroom communities of practice (Lave and Wenger, 1991; Wenger, 1998) where students can learn academic and critical literacies as their participation changes over time in sociocultural activities, such as the critical investigation of popular culture. Further, the chapter offers practical steps that all teachers can take to increase their awareness and understanding of popular culture. It is in this chapter that I promote the idea that teachers should become cultural anthropologists who use ethnography to learn about students' literate lives and involvement with popular culture outside of the classroom. I make several suggestions for how teachers can function as ethnographers even in the course of their normal, everyday activities.

The final section, *The Possibilities,* juxtaposes the myriad possibilities that popular culture offers against a current climate of standards, standardized tests, and censorship. Chapter 9 helps educators to see how the critical teaching of popular culture is highly compatible with state and national standards for literacy educators. This chapter acknowledges the recent focus, at the state and national levels, on standardized tests as the primary evaluator of academic skill. Within this context, the chapter provides a way for literacy educators to envision the practice of the teaching of popular culture that is commensurate with the current educational climate while also meeting various other goals, such as being culturally and socially relevant (Ladson-Billings, 1994). This chapter makes the case that literacy educators should be at the forefront of conversations about alternate forms of assessing students' literacy levels that are more compatible with recent developments in literacy studies and inclusive of students' non-school literacy practices, such as those associated with participation in popular culture.

Chapter 9 also tackles the sensitive issue of censorship and popular culture. Clearly, the inclusion of popular culture into traditional curricula will stir up a degree of controversy in even the most progressive of departments and schools, partly due to perceptions of it being vulgar, irreverent, or inappropriate for its primary consumers. In this chapter, I build upon arguments from chapter 2 that many of these misconceptions are contributable to a lack of knowledge about the breadth and scope of popular culture. I do, however, encourage teachers to be conservative in their initial forays into popular culture as I make the case that there is a wealth of valuable material to be used that should not raise any red flags. On the other hand, I also try to make the case that teachers need to encourage their colleagues to be consistent in evaluating the appropriateness of literary material across what they may categorize as elite and popular culture. Far too often, texts that are perceived as elite culture or classics are allowed into the curriculum though they contain many of the elements for which popular cultural texts are maligned.

Chapter 10 looks optimistically to a future where popular culture occupies a central role in literacy education and offers suggestions for teachers and teacher educators interested in making this future a reality. This chapter considers some of the implications of the research for classroom teaching, teacher education, and professional development. It offers a vision of the secondary literacy classroom that successfully incorporates popular culture while also teaching canonical literature and adhering to district, state, and national standards. It also provides insights for Teacher Education Programs, Master's Programs, and professional development seminars that aim to effectively prepare literacy educators to teach popular culture to America's youth.

The chapter and the book conclude with a call to action for teachers and teacher educators to position themselves as action researchers and activists who take ownership over the knowledge production and knowledge distribution within their own profession. Not only is it important for literacy educators and teacher educators to engage in innovative practices; we also need to perform research that is centered in the classroom and then find multiple ways to share this research with our colleagues, whether this takes the shape of a presentation to a department meeting, a research article, a conference presentation, or even a book like this one. I also contend that, in order to bring about the revolutionary instruction that this book advocates, teachers need to see themselves as activists and advocates for their students' interests and their own intellectual freedom as competent and creative professionals. In the end, what I hope is to have offered realistic and grounded, yet encouraging, words to teachers and teacher educators, suggesting that there are ways to meet these challenges that the new century offers and turn these challenges into opportunities to connect to the worlds of students, to promote academic achievement, and to prepare students for critical citizenship in a multicultural democracy.

Chapter 2

What Is Popular Culture?

Popular culture is a term that we all use, but seldom define. In fact, I will argue that the lack of definition often has educators and theorists talking past each other while using similar terms. Though a "popular" term, the "popular" definition of popular culture often ignores many of the conflicts and complexities that make popular culture such an important site of study for teachers and students. In this chapter I consider what English educators can learn from having a theoretical framework and historical introduction to popular culture. To do this means tramping through the tricky terrain of cultural theory. Some of the arguments may seem illusive and circular; but so, too, is the popular culture that permeates our lives and, more importantly, the lives of the students we teach. It is a worthwhile journey, I believe, for the educators who want to begin to gain the firm understanding of popular culture that I argue is needed for effective teaching, and for critical citizenship.

To these ends, this chapter explores critical and cultural theory to provide a grounded, yet accessible definition of popular culture for teachers and teacher educators. I begin by providing basic definitions of culture and popular culture that have emerged from cultural studies over the last half of the 20th century. I then outline the chronological development of popular culture and cultural studies in the 20th century, beginning with the Frankfurt School of Social Research, then moving to the Birmingham Centre for Contemporary Cultural Studies, and finally to popular culture and cultural studies in the American context. Within the American context, I examine several frameworks for understanding popular culture ranging from quantitative audience counts to the ideological struggle between local cultures and the media conglomerates that seek to capture and market them. I conclude by discussing the importance of English teachers developing a broad understanding of the origins and development of popular culture and cultural theory.

Popular Culture in the 20th Century

Popular Culture and the Frankfurt School of Social Research

The Frankfurt School is a name given to a collaborative of philosophers, sociologists, and literary theorists who began working together at the University of Frankfurt in the late 1920s. This school's combination of Marxism and psychoanalysis ultimately became known as critical theory. The Frankfurt School sociologists borrowed from Marx the idea that modern society was the site of struggle between two economic classes, the bourgeoisie (property-owning class) and the proletariat (working-class) (Marx, 1973). A core tenet of Marxist thought is that the bourgeoisie, through controlling the economic base of society, also controlled the cultural institutions promoting a consciousness (ideology) that promoted its interest. Workers, and other members of oppressed groups, would embrace this ideology (false consciousness) and, therefore, accept a set of relations that were counter to its interest. Marx's primary institution of focus was the workplace, but other Marxists would expand this analysis to include other social institutions such as schools and the media.

Further, Marxists theorists, such as Antonio Gramsci, would continue finding a language to explain how the overwhelming majority of people would accept a system that oppressed them without revolting against that system. Gramsci pushed upon Marx's idea of ideology as false consciousness and added another term, *hegemony*, which simply referred to the strategies, ideas, and beliefs that the dominant class would promote in order to manufacture consent among subordinate classes. It becomes easy to see how these theorists would maintain that schools and the media were key institutions that promoted the hegemony of the dominant classes.

It is important to understand that, in order for hegemony to be effective, it must appear, not as a set of contestable ideas, but as absolute and unquestioned fact. Marxist theorists like Gramsci and the Frankfurt School members felt that the ruling classes in Western societies were quite successful in promoting a set of ideas and values that maintained power in the hands of a precious few to the detriment of the overwhelming majority. The Frankfurt School theorists, however, felt that the most effective way to contest the hegemony of the dominant classes was to promote *critical theory*. Rather than accept any knowledge as absolute, critical theorists assumed that all knowledge was ideological and, therefore, sought to unpack the inherent power relations in all knowledge, asking constantly whose interests were being served and at what cost.

One of the initial targets of the critical theorists was the emergent popular culture or what Max Horkheimer and Ted Adorno, two of the most famous Frankfurt School theorists, termed the *culture industries*. At the risk of minimizing a rather complex argument, Adorno and Horkheimer believed that the culture industries (which would include popular music, film, television, and print media) were tools by which the dominant classes could standardize art and culture, thereby constraining critical thought and controlling the actions of the masses. Horkheimer and Adorno, indeed all of the Frankfurt theorists, were German Jews experiencing the onset of Hitler's Nazism, which ultimately forced them into exile in the United States. They saw firsthand how media culture could be used as propaganda to sway the public mood which, in less than a decade, was ready to stand idly by to witness Hitler's Final Solution. Horkheimer and Adorno would argue, however, that media propaganda was not limited to Nazi Germany. They identified many of the same effects of the culture industries during their extended stay in the United States.

Adorno, especially, devoted his career to the explanation of the ill effects of mass consumption of popular music, television, and film (Adorno, 1991). Throughout the 20th century, his work has been interpreted in various ways—negatively by those who felt that he was overreacting, and some, such as the Birmingham cultural theorists, who saw him as a visionary. However, with the recent proliferation of the media into people's lives, Adorno's work is as relevant and well received as it ever was. While I certainly see more positive aspects of popular culture than did Adorno, the initial discussion of the relationship between mainstream media and social attitudes has been central to my study of popular culture as well as my teaching. Other theorists in the British and American Cultural Studies movements would deal with the tensions surrounding the role of popular culture in society, but Adorno's critiques have never left the field.

Popular Culture and the Birmingham Centre for Contemporary Cultural Studies

British Cultural Studies emerged in the 1950s in response to Leavism, which was a form of literary criticism that advocated for a limited literary canon that excluded modern, popular works. The original founders of cultural studies, all from working-class backgrounds, rejected the idea that the only valuable knowledge was the literary tradition of the elite. Instead, Raymond Williams, Richard Hoggart, and Stuart Hall sought to develop a tradition that celebrated the everyday mass culture of the working-class that was denigrated in elite social contexts and in dominant social institutions, such as schools. Richard Hoggart's famous book *The Uses of Literacy* (1958), for example, celebrates the industrial, working-class communities of his youth. Hoggart would go on to found the Birmingham Centre for Contemporary Cultural Studies (CCCS), a place to engage in the study of mass culture.

One of the key differences between the Frankfurt School and the Birmingham Centre is the location of popular culture. While Adorno and Horkeimer located popular culture in the works of the culture industries, Hoggart, Hall, and Williams located popular culture in the everyday activities of working-class peoples. Whereas the Frankfurt theorists saw popular culture as a tool for social control, the British cultural theorists saw popular culture as a celebration and site of resistance. For the moment, it is not necessary to pick one or the other of the schools as being right or wrong. Rather, I think it important to understand how, together, they reveal a fundamental tension in cultural theory and the study of popular culture—that the same culture that represents working-class resistance can also be marketed to reinforce social inequality. These tensions and struggles are not only played out in the halls of the academy, they are part and parcel of modern life. For now, it is only important to recognize the two sides to this discussion of popular culture as each having something important to offer to educators interested in teaching popular culture. With that said, I would like to flesh out the definition of culture offered by one of the original British theorists, Raymond Williams, as a way of grounding a working definition of popular culture that will be developed further in this chapter and continually throughout the book.

Raymond Williams, in *Sociology of Culture*, offers a historical analysis of the social organization of culture in terms of its institutions and formations. Although his own background is in literary criticism, Williams asserts that the term sociology of culture implies a convergence of various interests and methods. With respect to literary criticism, Williams helped to move conversations from a restricted high culture to a notion of culture as ordinary—as a way of life or structure of feeling lived and experienced by the vast majority of people in a given society. He traces the evolution of culture through its various historical conditions toward a "complete" form. Williams sees the emergence of a general human culture in specific societies where it is shaped by local and temporary systems. Williams examines language in all of the forms in which it has been used to give meaning to lived experience. He argues that there is no such thing as the masses, only ways of seeing people as masses. Mass or ordinary culture can be good or bad, but the practice of assigning value can be tied to existing ideological structures that hold ordinary people, their efforts, and their artifacts in contempt.

Williams demonstrated that the concept of culture had come into existence as a holistic protest against the fragmenting effects of industrialism, and he strongly suggested that both "ordinary" culture and "the best that has been known and thought" therefore belonged to a common heritage of opposition. Williams begins the book by explaining the relationship between cultural studies and market research. He uses examples from medieval Welsh culture to offer a precapital counterpoint to contemporary relations between the artist and society where, in his estimation, art is dependent on market forces. Williams, however, works to dismiss his earlier notions that the market is an impenetrable enemy of cultural critics and sociologists. He employs popular culture as an example of a generally oppositional cultural form that can be produced in and by, rather than outside and against, capitalist consumerism. He further suggests that the sociology of culture be used to blur the lines between the cultural critic and the military/industrial technician and shows how critics must work from within the systems that they define themselves against. In this book Williams looks forward to the birth of a new major discipline that would deal with culture very differently and begins to lay the theoretical groundwork for this new Cultural Studies. He makes several recommendations for a sociology of culture:

1. It is concerned with the social processes of all cultural production, including the forms of production that can be designated as ideologies;

2. It must concern itself with the institutions and formations of cultural production;

3. It must concern itself with the social relations of its specific means of production;

4. It must concern itself with specific artistic forms (i.e., hip-hop music);

5. It must concern itself with the processes of social and cultural reproduction; and

6. It must concern itself with general and specific problems of cultural organization.

Like Adorno, the work of the CCCS continues to be interpreted, even as it continues to evolve. The work of American cultural studies, for example, has drawn heavily upon the CCCS and, particularly, the work of Hoggart, Williams, and Hall to develop a field to study the emergence and ascendance of subcultures (i.e., cyberpunk, rock music culture, gangs, youth culture, etc.) while also relying on the work inspired by the Frankfurt theorists to study the nature of the relations between popular media and the masses that consume them. Further, American cultural theorists have considered the importance of cultural studies to primary and secondary education. With this in mind, it is to the American theorists that I now turn.

Popular Culture in American Cultural Studies and Educational Research

John Docker, in *Postmodernism and Popular Culture: A Cultural History* (1994), questions the way a century of modernist critical theory has made sense of 20th century mass culture and suggests that postmodernism may promise more illuminating approaches. Modernism, he feels, has demonized mass culture as the chief danger to civilization. Postmodernism, on the other hand, does not ascribe to popular cultural phenomena any single commanding meaning or purpose. In other words, Docker does not ascribe any grand narrative of popular culture and its impact on society. His postmodern theory of popular culture does not assume any easily explicable relationship between popular culture and its audiences, and it does not see audiences as transparent in their desires and consciousness, as does the work of Adorno in many respects. His concept of popular culture also does not assign a hierarchy of genres in culture in general. Postmodernism, rather, is interested in a plurality of forms and genres, a pluralizing of aesthetic criteria, and a respect for the interacting, conflicting, and contested histories of these genres. Postmodernism sees popular culture as a frequent site of flamboyance, extravagance, excess, parody, and self-parody, as well as a site of resistance.

In utilizing postmodern theory to make sense of popular culture, Docker is able to imagine a popular culture that does not land on any of the poles mentioned in earlier sections. Rather than view popular culture as worthy of celebration or denigration, Docker, and many of the American cultural theorists attempt to describe the multiple, conflicting purposes of popular culture in contemporary society. This will be an important theme throughout the units that I discuss in chapters 4 through 7. I agree with Docker that popular culture plays multiple, conflicting, and even contradictory roles in the lives of our youth. I also believe that the more young people are given opportunities to explore these various roles, the better consumers and producers of popular culture they'll be. Docker's postmodern perspective of popular culture allows educators to talk about popular culture in ways that affirm and celebrate students' non-school lives, while also providing the language and tools to make sense of how popular culture can serve to constrain, limit, marginalize, reproduce negative attitudes, and help to maintain social inequality.

Storey, in *An Introduction to Cultural Theory and Popular Culture* (1998), provides an introduction to the academic study of popular culture. He begins by struggling to define what he feels is a vacuous term conceptually. Popular culture, he asserts, is always defined implicitly or explicitly, in contrast to other conceptual categories such as folk culture, mass culture, or dominant culture. He offers, however, six definitions of popular culture that will be used in later analyses:

1. Popular culture is culture that is well liked by many people;
2. Popular culture is what remains after we have decided what is high culture (the notion of popular culture as substandard culture);
3. Popular culture is mass culture;
4. Popular culture is that culture which originates from the people;
5. Popular culture is inspired by neo-Gramscian hegemony theory; and

6. Popular culture can be viewed through the lens of postmodernism that no longer recognizes the distinction between high and popular culture.

Hegemony, again, for Gramsci is a political concept developed to explain the absence of socialist revolutions in Western capitalist democracies. The concept of hegemony is used by Gramsci to refer to a process in which a dominant class does not merely rule a society, but leads it through the exercise of moral and intellectual leadership. In this sense, the concept is used to suggest a society in which, despite oppression and exploitation, there is a high degree of consensus and a large measure of social stability—a society in which the subordinate groups and classes appear to support meanings that bind them to, and incorporate them into, the prevailing structures of power. Hegemony is organized by those that Gramsci designates the *organic intellectuals*.

In this approach, popular culture is seen as a site of struggle between the forces of resistance of subordinate groups in society, and the forces of incorporation of dominant groups in society. Popular culture in this usage is not an imposed "mass culture," or a "people's culture," it is more of a terrain of exchange between the two. The texts and practices of popular culture move within what Gramsci calls a "compromise equilibrium." Those who look at popular culture from a neo-Gramscian perspective tend to see it as a terrain of ideological struggle between dominant and subordinate classes, or dominant and subordinate cultures. Using a neo-Gramscian analysis, popular culture is what men and women make from their active consumption of the texts and practices of the culture industries. Youth cultures, for example, are able to appropriate for their own purposes and meanings the commodities that are commercially provided. For instance, in popular musical genres such as Reggae and hip-hop, it is possible to have anti-capitalist politics articulated in the economic interests of capitalism. The music may be lubricating the very system that it seeks to condemn. It may exist as an expression of oppositional politics that produces certain political and cultural effects in a form that is of financial benefit to the dominant culture. Cultural theorists must be aware of the simultaneous possibilities of the making of popular culture for subordinate groups. It has the potential of empowerment and resistance, but it can also lead to passivity and consumption of the hegemonic ideals promoted by the organic intellectuals of the dominant class. Popular culture has also been the object of a great deal of (Radical/

Marxist/Liberal) feminist analysis. Cultural politics are crucially important to feminism because they involve struggles over (dominant/patriarchal/hegemonic) meanings.

Popular Culture is defined by McCarthy (1998) as, "the historically grounded experiences and practices of oppressed women and men and the processes by which these experiences and practices come to be represented, reconstructed, and reinvented in daily life, in school, in the workplace, and in the news media" (p. 38). Popular culture finds its expression through music, film, fashion, language, and the media. Frequently, popular culture has been discussed as common culture or juxtaposed against high or elite culture in a dichotomous fashion (Adorno and Horkheimer, 1999). McCarthy, however, joins Docker and Storey by situating popular culture in its resonance with oppressed groups while arguing for its position at the center of discussions of education and social change. This last point is extremely important because McCarthy is among the generation of American theorists who promote the study of popular culture as a mechanism for social change. For decades, critical and cultural theory had remained the domain of philosophers, sociologists, and other academicians interested in studying modern civilizations or media studies. McCarthy, however, makes the argument that teachers and students need to study popular culture in order to make sense of the world in socially empowering ways. It is important to note that this is also happening across the water; British cultural theorists are also arguing for media studies in their schools. However, while critical and cultural theory have thrived in philosophy, sociology, and literature departments in other nations, the American cultural theorists have frequently found homes in schools of education and have placed in the foreground the pedagogical applications of popular culture.

Henry Giroux is one of the American cultural theorists most responsible for bringing discussions of popular culture into the educational literature. In *Fugitive Cultures: Race, Violence, and Youth*, Giroux (1996) addresses the crisis confronting youth (whom he labels a generation under siege) where they are enmeshed in a culture of violence coded by race and class. He speaks to the negative connotations of youth culture promoted in popular media that propel youth toward mistrust, alienation, misogyny, violence, apathy, and the development of fugitive cultures. This same media has commercialized the working-class body and criminalized black youth. Giroux argues for a *critical media literacy* (Kellner, 1995) in schools where teachers consider popular media, film, and music as serious sites for social knowledge to be discussed, interrogated, and critiqued. Whether the power in its messages can be used for good or ill, few, he argues, can dispute the impact of popular culture in the lives of working-class, urban youth. Giroux promotes a synthesis of critical pedagogy and cultural studies to gain a critical understanding of how youth are being constructed differently within a popular culture that is simultaneously oppressive and resistant and represents violence as a legitimate practice to define youth identity.

Mahiri (1998) utilizes these critical and cultural theories to examine the curricular practices of urban teachers. He contends that teachers can become sources of resistance to the ideology and practices of cultural domination and exploitation that permeate institutional structures in this society by working to better understand and build on the authentic experiences of students who have been marginalized by the educational process. This can be achieved by the creation of counter-hegemonic curricula. By counter-hegemonic curricula, Mahiri simply means lessons and units that explicitly challenge dominant norms, practices, and assumptions that may be detrimental to students, their families, and their communities.

Mahiri draws on findings from four research projects to suggest ways that classroom discourse, curricula, and culture can be changed to enhance processes of teaching and learning by building more powerfully on the authentic experiences of students. His study considers African American culture and youth or popular culture as sites for which young people have forged a common identity manifested in dress, language use, music, video games, and common heroes. Mahiri argues that aspects of popular culture can act as unifying and equalizing forces in culturally diverse classrooms and that African American and youth cultural sources for curricula can motivate learning of traditional subject matter as well.

Giroux and Mahiri have been important in laying the groundwork for the serious study of popular culture in America's classrooms. After the important and difficult conceptual groundwork had been laid, I tried to develop long-term studies that might shed light on what instruction utilizing popular culture might look like in classrooms. I wanted to consider the impact on literacy achievement, while also considering effects on personal identity and commitment to social change. Further, I wanted to understand what this would mean for the educators interested in such an enterprise. In many ways, I have endeavored to bring the conversations initiated by Adorno, Horkheimer, Hoggart, Hall, Williams, Giroux, and Mahiri into actual classrooms for the explicit purposes of transforming classroom instruction, student literacy practices, and, ultimately, playing a small role in transforming our world. I am encouraging you to do the same.

Why English Teachers Need a Framework for Understanding Popular Culture

This may seem like a great deal to digest. After all, I have only truncated a century's worth of critical philosophy and cultural theory into a tiny, but robust chapter. I sincerely believe that the preceding journey was a worthwhile one for any educators who want to bring popular culture into their curricular offerings. I argue that it is important for English teachers to develop a broad understanding of the history and development of popular culture for a number of important reasons. I have listed some of the more pertinent ones below:

1. Developing a broad conceptual framework for popular culture and cultural studies will help teachers make the case for the inclusion of popular culture into traditional literacy curricula in moving beyond popular culture as a collection of student-oriented media texts and re-casting popular culture as the representation of everyday activity. This re-casting also repositions young people as producers and participants in popular culture, rather than as passive consumers of popular culture.

2. An understanding of the history and frameworks for popular culture helps teachers to understand and contend against the negative reactions to teaching popular culture in classrooms.

3. Being exposed to this historical background and conceptual framework broadens the scope of what teachers might do when teaching popular culture. Hopefully, we can move beyond literary analyses of mainstream media texts to make connections to students' lived experiences in the world.

4. A solid background in critical and cultural theories creates a generative knowledge base that potentially leads to discussions between teachers and students about popular culture as a simultaneous site of resistance to and co-optation by the culture industries. Further, this framework also allows teachers to help students understand how their everyday practices are also

considered popular culture and often inform the cultural products promoted and marketed by the culture industries.

5. A background in cultural theory, particularly Williams's sociology of culture, provides teachers and students with a more sophisticated conception of culture that moves beyond simplified, monoracial identities. This is important in ethnically diverse classes to help students understand that culture is more than ethnicity and that persons of different ethnicities can share common cultures—an important first step in a true "multicultural" curriculum.

6. A broad understanding of the many facets of popular culture legitimates the study of countercultures and subcultures in the English classroom. This opens up spaces for students to engage in independent study projects of cultural practices within their own communities.

This is only a limited list of the many benefits that teachers may accrue from gaining a conceptual and historical understanding of popular culture, which I now hope that you have. Chapter 3 contains nothing but reasons why teachers should consider using popular culture in their classrooms. For now, I hope that your interest has been piqued and your grounding in the terminology solidified. At the very least, I hope you feel inspired to get through chapter 3 before jumping into the teaching of music, film, media, and sports.

The Case for Popular Culture in America's Classrooms

Chapter 1 sought to outline the myriad of challenges that English teachers face in 21st–century classrooms. It also introduced the notion of popular culture as part of a set of strategies to confront these challenges. Chapter 2, then provided a historical background and outlined a theoretical explanation of popular culture. Building upon these ideas, this chapter articulates a rationale for teachers to consider incorporating popular culture in their classrooms to promote academic achievement and critical consciousness among their students. This comprehensive annotated list covers a wide range of possible social, cultural, and intellectual impacts for individual students, teachers, and the classroom community as a whole. This chapter outlines several arguments, including: popular culture is relevant to the lives of adolescents; popular culture is imbedded with relevant literacy practices; popular culture can help students make connections to academic texts and concepts; and popular culture fosters greater motivation among students. It is to these arguments that I now turn.

Popular Culture Is Relevant to the Lives of Adolescents

There are several ways to look at the issue of "relevance" as it pertains to the teen-agers who find themselves in secondary English classrooms. First, relevance can be measured quantitatively, by the sheer amount of involvement with popular culture. Related studies that have attempted to quantify the nature of adolescent engagement with popular culture have measured television viewing patterns, demographic analyses of box office attendance, and volume of compact discs and popular magazines sold to youth. A second way to look at relevance is thematically; that is, that the topics and themes of the movies, songs, magazines, web sites, and television shows reflect the lived experiences of the students that we teach. I'd like to talk about each of these in more detail.

Almost from the beginning of media studies as a discipline, researchers have been interested in the consumption habits of children and teens (Casey et al., 2002). There is no doubt, for instance, that teens are a major target of television programming with whole networks such as Nickelodeon, the Disney Channel, and MTV (Music television) catering to children and teens. There are also many prime time shows such as *Party of Five* and *South Park* that cater to youth and offer a portrait of a youth culture that is independent of, if not in opposition, to the adult world.

This same trend exhibits itself in the film industry with teen-angst films such as *American Pie, Freaky Friday, Scary Movie, Spiderman,* and *Lizzy McGuire* grossing millions of dollars at the box office. The science fiction genre, with films such as the *Harry Potter,* and *Lord of the Rings* series, set box office records while targeting adolescent audiences (Corey and Ochoa, 2002). A recent issue of *Vanity Fair* highlighted the teens that are taking over Hollywood. Not only are the major stars getting younger, so too are the major consumers in America's theaters.

Farley (1999) documents this trend in the music industry in his *Time* magazine article that traces the ascendancy of hip-hop music and culture. In the "hip-hop nation" Farley reveals, over 80 million CDs are sold annually to waiting fans that are mostly teens, more than for any other genre of music. The consensus of these reports is abundantly clear; America's teens are saturated with popular culture as they are the major producers and consumers, both in time and money, of popular media. As such, they are also the major targets of corporate popular cultural production, programming, and advertisements.

Several cultural theorists have sought to understand how texts of popular culture relate thematically with the lives of today's youth (Giroux, 1996; Lipsitz, 1994). In fact, much of the popular cultural production through mainstream media is at once a reflection of youth experience and an inspiration for it. It is important for educators to understand both sides of this issue. On one side, youth's everyday experiences are the material of popular culture. Some of this material is gleaned from adults who claim to be "in the know" or who know which young people to hire as informants to test products or services that cater to youth interests. Most of the material, however, is produced by the youth themselves in the form of garage bands, street linguists, and closet seamstresses who take it upon themselves to remake cultures in their image. Whole genres and youth movements such as hip-hop have come into existence via the creativity and genius of young women and men attempting to find modes expressing their rich and complicated lives. For obvious reasons, these cultural products are relevant; they are actual creations by youth themselves who know, more than anyone, what it means to be in their shoes.

Not all of the artifacts associated with youth subcultures become commercialized; most garage bands are never signed and most street fashion is never incorporated by corporate brands. These local artifacts, however, remain important in their relation to commercialized products and the everyday practices of young people as they interact with their culture that is marketed to them by the culture industries. The other side of the coin, quite simply, is that major corporations are the primary definers and determinants of youth popular culture. Although the material may originate with youth, it is ultimately executives in tall office buildings who will decide what the latest brand of Nike shoes is going to look like or which "grunge" band is going to get the contract and the nationwide tour. The two sides are not exclusive of one another and do not detract from the argument that whether they are the producers or consumers, popular culture plays a central role in dictating how youth define themselves in relation to the larger world as well as framing their practices (i.e., dress, speech, or recreational activities) within that larger world.

It is important to note that many adults would consider the affects of youth interactions with much popular culture as negative and detrimental to self-esteem and to value formation. Henry Giroux, for instance, decries the treatment of working-class youth in popular film and television. According to Giroux, African American males are often criminalized in popular culture while working-class bodies of young women and men are commodified in these same arenas. This is certainly true of my experiences watching many films and television shows; it doesn't require much critical faculties to understand that young women and men are portrayed in problematic ways in television and film.

I will reiterate throughout the book, however, that I am not encouraging teachers and researchers to celebrate all aspects of popular youth, though many aspects are worthy of celebration. Instead, the goal is to make clear the ascendancy of popular culture in the lives of America's youth, both in terms of volume and significance of exposure. Given the comments of cultural theorists such as Giroux, or even my own analysis, it is safe to argue that teachers would do well to enable their students to read against the texts that they consume in such mass quantities even as they learn a discourse that enables them to appreciate the source and content of the texts as being their own lived experiences in the social world.

Popular Cultural Consumption Involves Intellectually Rigorous Literacy Practices

A second worthy argument is that popular culture involves intellectually rigorous literate activity. Many educators and policymakers have long held that there exists a distinction between popular culture and elite culture, obviously deciding to focus on the latter given its superior rigor, content, and worth to humanity. This attitude finds its way into America's secondary classrooms as well. I would like to challenge these assumptions by offering that popular cultural consumption and production are intellectual activities that coordinate with the goals of secondary English teaching.

Young people are involved in many rigorous and relevant literacy activities that are related to their participation in youth popular culture. For instance, there are a host of important literate activities associated with students' participation as consumers and producers of popular music. Students who are interested in popular music often purchase magazines such as *Vibe, Spin,* and *Rolling Stone* that feature well-written articles that cover the music industry and its practitioners. The featured critiques of musical texts and performances are strikingly similar to the literary analyses that teachers want from their secondary students. In fact, it is more likely that students will read more exposition via their participation in popular culture than they actually would in classrooms that frequently assess knowledge of fictional texts through non-fictional expository writing. In addition to literary critiques of musical artists and texts, contemporary fashion, and popular culture in general, these periodicals also cover issues of national if not international concern. It is not uncommon for popular cultural magazines to feature interviews with famous politicians to discuss prominent world events. For example, a recent edition of *Rolling Stone* magazine featured a series of articles discussing media bias in the representation of the confrontation between the United States and Iraq; and a recent edition of *Vibe* featured a critique of Hollywood's co-optation of hip-hop music and culture. These critical media readings, targeted primarily toward adolescents, mirror the type of critical approach to texts that teachers expect of their students at the secondary and postsecondary levels. A teacher interested in teaching critical media studies need look no further than popular magazines for abundant sources of analysis and critique.

Students also are involved in a great deal of Internet activity in relation to their love of popular music. Some key examples include: searching industry sites for information on particular groups or musicians running fan web sites and chat rooms, downloading mpeg files and lyrics, and searching for concert tickets. These cyberliterate activities force adolescents to develop reading, writing, and research skills that would serve them well in academic subjects and in their futures as working professionals and engaged citizens. They also develop cyberliteracy skills that have even adult executives baffled. For example, no matter what the music industry attempts, it cannot prevent the capture and free-flowing exchange of commercialized musical content on the Internet. America's teens are able to break through complex encryption codes and develop mechanisms for consuming and distributing digital music with virtual impunity (no pun intended).

Finally, many young people are composers and producers of popular cultural texts. These young men and women carry volumes of notebooks containing original song lyrics and poems. They are wont to spontaneously compose on envelopes, napkins, folders, desks, and, yes, sometimes walls. They share lyrics and poetry with peers who are also aspiring artists. They post their philosophies and life histories on web sites and, more recently, web logs (blogs). They even participate in cyberactivism, circulating petitions and news releases about injustice around the world. It has been largely teens who have created massive virtual networks for activists to share information and collaborate all over the world. Online activists, for example, have staged international protests against the World Bank and buoyed local indigenous struggles such as that of the Zapatista movement in Chiapas, Mexico (McCaughey and Ayers, 2003). Hackers and code breakers have also engaged in electronic civil disobedience against major multinational corporations (Meikle, 2002; Sterling, 1992).

Unfortunately, most of this activity occurs outside of the gaze of classroom teachers, who could tap into this massive textual production and assist these burgeoning artists, intellectuals, entrepreneurs, and activists. Often the students who do the most writing outside of school are the aspiring musicians and filmmakers, the hackers, and the media activists. More than once, I have seen teachers presume students who are engaged in tremendous amounts of reading and writing related to their artistic pursuits are semiliterate or not interested in such literary pursuits when most of these students' voluntary activities can be described as literacy based.

Teaching Popular Culture can Help Young People Make Connections to Academic Texts and Concepts

One of the most basic and fundamental of ideas to all of contemporary educational psychology is Vygotsky's (1978) concept of the Zone of Proximal Development. For nearly half a century, educators in the West have taken refuge in the idea of using students' strengths and background experiences as starting points to scaffold ideas and concepts that would otherwise be beyond their reach. Vygotsky, a Russian psychologist who lived during the first half of the 20th century, believed that learning is inherently social, that it usually involves mentoring from more culturally knowledgeable persons, and that meaning is constructed through joint activity. Carol Lee and Peter Smagorinsky's introductory chapter to their edited volume *Vygotskian Perspectives on Literacy Research* (2000) and Luis Moll's introductory chapter to his edited book *Vygotsky in Education* (1990) are excellent background sources for those interested in knowing more about Vygotsky and his ideas about the social nature of learning.

Vygotsky's psychology is important for teachers who are struggling to make meaningful connections with their students. His theories about learning—along with those sociocultural psychologists who have been inspired by him such as Michael Cole, Kris Gutierrez, Jean Lave, Carol Lee, Luis Moll, Barbara Rogoff, and Sylvia Scribner—have led the way for educators to begin curriculum with the needs of the student and not the parameters of the content area or the standards of the discipline. This important shift can lead to more innovative practices, such as the infusing of music, film, mass media, and sports into traditional secondary English curricula, along with a set of activities that allow students to acquire literacy skills as they participate in socially meaningful contexts.

There is one caveat in drawing upon Vygotsky and sociocultural psychology however. In the earlier chapters, I contend strongly against the argument that popular culture is a safe and easy way into the more rigorous and challenging ideas presented in classical texts and standard curricula. For years, popular culture has stood in this relation to the more elite culture that has been the backbone of English curriculum. It would be against the interests of this book if teachers felt that popular cultural texts were a stepping stone to more intellectual texts and concepts that appear on advanced placement tests and college syllabi. In fact, such an attitude would do more harm than good. There is a generation of research started by multiculturalists such as James Banks and Sonia Nieto that have warned against the negative impacts on self-esteem, motivation, and achievement associated with the denigration and marginalization of students' home cultures in America's classrooms. Nieto (1996) encourages teachers to take steps to affirm and celebrate student diversity. I would hope that idea extended to youth culture and not just students' ethnic and linguistic heritages.

This book, on the other hand, makes the argument that the move from popular to classical/traditional is more one from proximity to distance than it is from the simple to the complex. That is, once students have learned to make sense of the texts that permeate their own world, they will be better able to engage the texts that represent the languages, cultures, and experiences of worlds distant and past.

Popular Culture Can Facilitate a Critical Reading(s) of the Worlds of America's Youth

John Dewey, in the *School and Society* (1903/1956), has spoken to the multiple purposes of school—chiefly, the preparation of future professionals and the preparation of future citizens of a multicultural democracy. Over time, however, it seems as if the latter purpose has waned in importance. The increasing literacy demands of a technology-focused economy have asked more and more of school curricula in the preparation of workers who are able to contribute to a rapidly changing and globalizing economy. This shift in focus leads to the unfortunate exclusion of civic education, which is needed more than ever, given these changes and the interesting, yet unique juxtaposition of diverse individuals that they precipitate.

Even this book has been remiss up to this point, in grounding its argument in the ability of teaching popular culture to increasing academic achievement and, by association, preparation for professional employment. Such a focus is justified, given the importance of academic and professional literacies to the lives and livelihoods of our students. I do, however, believe that it is within the scope of literacy education to help future professionals consider how their actions or inactions either mitigate or contribute to a more just and equitable global order. In that spirit, I now want to momentarily leave the academic-focused argument to consider the benefits of teaching popular culture to creating a critical and engaged citizenry.

It is no secret that popular culture saturates the lives of America's youth and, indeed, its citizens of all ages. One of the definitions of popular culture emanates from the sheer volume of interaction. As you may recall, several cultural theorists have justifiably made the argument that popular culture plays a major role in developing youth's sense of identity. Popular culture is also the source from which these young people receive the overwhelming majority of information about themselves as subjects situated within the social world. Several philosophers of culture (Adorno and Horkheimer, 1999; Kellner, 1995; Lipsitz, 1994) have spoken to the negative outcomes associated with an uncritical consumption of popular culture for America's youth, such as low self-image and reinforced stereotypical norms for gender and ethnic groups. Uncritical consumption of popular culture can also lead to, well, uncritical consumption. Major corporations use popular culture to create a consumer base that becomes dependent on their products. By the end of any given day, young people can feel as if they are ugly, uncool, overweight, or unaccepted if they do not constantly buy the latest and most "popular" products. Worse yet, consumption or overconsumption can lead to many of these same problems, as evidenced by the increasing percentage of America's teens who are overweight largely attributable to the consumption of fatty and sugary foods that are targeted to them through popular media and even advertised on school campuses. Additionally, feelings of angst, depression, and even domestic disputes are aroused with the increasing gap between what material products America's teens feel they need and what their struggling families can afford.

Critically teaching popular culture can go a long way in creating an informed and engaged citizenry of young people that are able to more carefully discern and interact with the messages that bombard them on a daily basis. Gaining an understanding of media bias and consumer culture will help students become more informed and discerning consumers at this most important time in their lives. These ideas, more commonly referred to as critical media literacy, are discussed in more detail in chapter 6, which is completely devoted to developing classroom curricula to foster critical media reading.

Another important reason to critically teach popular culture to teens is the presence of powerful themes of resistance and social critique contained within many popular texts. Going back to the Civil Rights Movement and the Vietnam War era, popular cultural texts have played a major role in outlining and educating the public sphere about oppressive and inequitable conditions at home and abroad. Films, songs, television broadcasts, and print media publications with a countercultural bent have been central in changing attitudes and galvanizing citizens to become participants in movements geared toward social change. Introducing our youth to the power of popular cultural texts to change the world is also an important part of creating critical and engaged citizens. Chapters 4, 5, and 7 speak at length to this potential of teaching popular culture.

At this point, it probably makes most sense to be specific about the *critical teaching* advocated in this teaching of popular culture. Having a powerful curriculum without a correspondingly powerful teaching approach will fail to achieve the academic or social results expressed in this book. In fact, I would go so far as to argue that, without the appropriate teaching approach, it is impossible to have a powerful and engaging curriculum. Therefore, it is the intent of this book that beginning and experienced practitioners see themselves as critical teachers of popular culture to adolescents in secondary schools.

Critical Pedagogy and Popular Culture

Just what is critical pedagogy and why is it important for those interested in using popular culture to facilitate literacy development? Although it is variously defined, critical pedagogy is linked to relationships between teachers, students, and communities that facilitate empowerment and transformation of the self and the social. As I have illustrated in chapter 2, popular culture is essentially a site of struggle between everyday people and institutions of power, such as the corporate media. Any attempts to teach or incorporate popular culture without acknowledging power runs the risk of reinforcing oppressive power relations and alienating young people from their own experiences. Certainly, the acquisition of academic literacy is empowering, but meaningless without access to enabling narratives of the self in the world. Critical pedagogy is about allowing students to reinsert themselves as subjects in their own narratives as opposed to being the objects of dominant ones. Such a process requires teachers to step back and consider how their own attitudes toward popular culture and the "everyday citizens" whose lives are portrayed are shaped by their subordination to dominant narratives.

Max Horkheimer (1972), a German philosopher and critical theorist, asserts that critical theory is about constantly questioning existing relations as determining and determined by power relations; but it is also questioning and reflexive of itself as theory. Once it ceases to question itself, it ceases to function as critical theory. For the same reason, teachers can encourage their students to embrace this same stance toward knowledge production by embracing such a stance themselves. Critical educators can model the stance toward knowledge and the world they advocate by constantly and publicly questioning their practice, the project of schooling, popular culture, and power relations in society.

Those of us who teach literacy as a tool of resistance and social change are indebted to the work of critical pedagogists who have given us a language to describe and deconstruct structures of oppression in the cause of social justice. McLaren (1994) asserts that:

> Critical pedagogy challenges the assumption that schools function as major sites of social and economic mobility. Proponents of this pedagogical theory suggest that schooling must be analyzed as a cultural and historical process, in which select groups are positioned within asymmetrical relations of power on the basis of specific race, class, and gender groupings. (p. 166)

According to McLaren (1994), critical scholars reject the claim that schooling constitutes an apolitical and value-neutral process. Critical pedagogy attempts to provide teachers and researchers with a better means of understanding the role that schools actually play within a race-, class-, and gender-divided society. In this effort, theorists have generated categories or concepts for questioning student experiences, popular and canonical texts, teacher ideologies, and aspects of school policy that other analyses too often leave unexplored.

In her 1991 book *Culture and Power in the Classroom: A Critical Foundation for Bicultural Education*, Darder asserts that the core tenets of critical pedagogy are also conducive to the needs of bicultural students—students who must learn to function in two distinct sociocultural environments: their primary culture and that of the dominant mainstream culture in the society in which they live. Darder contends that a critical bicultural pedagogy:

Can create the conditions for bicultural students to develop the courage to question the structures of domination that control their lives. In this way, they can awaken their bicultural voice as they participate in opportunities to reflect, critique, and act together with other bicultural students who are also experiencing the same process of discovery. Hence, these students are not just provided with curricular content that is considered culturally appropriate and language instruction in their native tongues. Rather, they are actively involved in considering critically all curriculum content, texts, classroom experiences, and their own lives for the emancipatory as well as oppressive and contradictory values that inform their thoughts, attitudes and behaviors. Through this process, bicultural students develop their abilities to understand critically their lives and how to engage actively with the world. (p. 96)

From the work of philosophers and practitioners such as Freire, McLaren, and Darder, a generation of critical educators has been inspired to enact pedagogical practices that enable a bicultural, marginalized opposition to read and act against the interests of power while inspiring movements of change. These educators continue enhanced, but not halted or deterred, by certain postmodernists who rail against concepts such as critical consciousness or warn against adherence to any totalizing narratives, even narratives of resistance. They continue steadfast in the project of emancipation amid a contemporary moment pregnant with ultra-conservative tendencies and intellectuals paralyzed by doubt and angst. Rather than reciprocate dismissal, they advocate a critical pedagogy compatible with and even inclusive of postmodern critiques of earlier iterations of our discourse. Like Jameson (1999), these teacher-activists simultaneously pay serious attention to the warranted critiques of modern, Enlightenment thinking while holding fast to rhetorics of resistance.

Aronowitz and Giroux (1991) argue that the challenge of post-modernism is important for critical educators because it raises crucial questions regarding certain hegemonic aspects of modernism and, by implication, how these have affected the meaning and dynamics of present-day schooling. Postmodernist criticism is also important because it offers the promise of redrawing the political, social, and cultural boundaries of modernism while simultaneously affirming a politics of racial, gender, and ethnic difference. Moreover, postmodern criticism does not merely challenge dominant Western cultural models with their attendant notion of universally valid knowledge; it also resituates us within a world that bears little resemblance to the one that inspired the grand narratives of Marx and Freud. In effect, postmodern criticism calls attention to the shifting boundaries related to the increasing influence of the electronic mass media and information technology, the changing nature of class and social formations in postindustrialized capitalist societies, and the growing transgression of boundaries between life and art, high and popular culture, and image and reality. Aronowitz and Giroux ultimately argue for a critical postmodernism that develops forms of pedagogy that incorporate difference, plurality, and the language of the everyday as central to the production and legitimization of learning.

In a similar vein, McLaren (1994) advocates the construction of a politics of difference, derived from the framework of resistance postmodernism, which creates narratives of liberation and freedom that critique master narratives, yet doesn't disintegrate into chaos and fragmentation. He concludes by encouraging educators to take up the issue of difference in ways that don't reinforce notions of monocultural essentialism and to create politics of alliance that move beyond race awareness week. He also advocates a resistance postmodernism that takes multiculturalism seriously, calling attention to the dominant meaning systems readily available to students, most of which are ideologically stitched into the fabric of Western imperialism (p. 214). Finally, he calls for a critical pedagogy that provides both the conditions for interrogating the institutionalization of formal equality based on the imperatives of a white, Anglo-Saxon male world and for creating spaces to facilitate an investigation of the way in which dominant institutions can be transformed so they no longer reinforce indifference to victimization and asymmetrical relations of power and privilege.

This critical postmodern pedagogy opens up ample spaces for

critical educators interested in literacy instruction for social change. Critical pedagogy is, of course, fundamentally and intimately linked with critical literacy. There can be no liberation of self or other without tools or language to perform counter-readings of dominant texts that serve the interests of power. Freire (1970) remarks that acceptance of dehumanizing conditions is promoted via a banking metaphor of education in which teachers are charged to disseminate knowledge to passive and empty receptacles of students who then embrace problematic and subordinating logics that are passed on as neutral and natural maxims for life. Reading, in this model, is simply decoding messages sent by power brokers through hegemonic curricula and media narratives. Freire and Macedo (1987), by contrast, promote a framework for critical reading as a part of radical pedagogy that:

> . . . has as its goal to enable students to become critical of the hegemonic practices that have shaped their experiences and perceptions in hopes of freeing themselves from the bonds of these dominating ideologies. (p. 55)

These ideas are by no means new or unique. Many researchers and other advocates have argued from diverse perspectives that teachers need to learn from their students how best to teach them. Further, teachers have been considering for some time how to co-construct knowledge with their students. Critical pedagogy, however, is unique in its explicit attention to power relations, in its acknowledgement of schools as reproductive institutions, and in its identification of teaching as a political activity. Critical pedagogy offers an important heuristic and conceptual language for practitioners and researchers who see themselves as agents of change.

Apple (1990) argues that teaching is a political act and neutrality does not exist when it comes to education. Any attempts to teach the "standard" curriculum without question or critique are political because they implicitly support the interests and ideals of the dominant class. This work goes to great lengths to demonstrate how curricular choices, teaching styles, and approaches to "factual" disciplines like science and history all function to promote the continued superiority of the dominant class at the expense of the subordinated groups who, not only are more inclined to fail, but come to embrace and accept that failure. What Apple and other critical educational theorists promote is a counter-hegemonic curriculum that teaches these students to question what has been accepted as fact and also to question their present condition in school and in society. In *Cultural Politics and Education* (1996), Apple makes the argument that part of reconceiving official knowledge and creating a curriculum of resistance entails the usage of elements of popular culture:

> Anything "popular" is soiled. It is not quite serious knowledge. Because of this, too often we assume that popular literature, popular culture, popular mathematics and science are failed knowledge. It is not quite real. Popular knowledge is pathologized, at least in comparison to the existing academic curriculum, which is seen as uplifting and neutral. Yet the existing curriculum is never a neutral assemblage of knowledge . . . we should know by now that popular culture is partly a site of resistance and struggle, but also that for schooling to make a difference it must connect to popular understandings and cultural forms. (p. 95)

Giroux (1996) addresses the crisis confronting youth, where they are enmeshed in a culture of violence coded by race and class. He speaks to the negative connotations of youth culture promoted in popular media that propel youth toward mistrust, alienation, misogyny, violence, apathy, and the development of fugitive cultures. Giroux argues for critical media literacy in schools where critical pedagogists consider popular media, film, and music as serious sites for social knowledge to be discussed, interrogated, and critiqued. Whether the power in its messages can be used for good or ill, few, he argues can dispute the impact of popular culture in the lives of working-class, urban youth. Giroux promotes a synthesis of critical pedagogy and cultural studies to gain a critical understanding of how youth are being constructed differently within a popular culture that is simultaneously oppressive and resistant and represents violence as a legitimate practice to define youth identity.

My reading of the critical and cultural theorists that I cite above corroborate my own experiences to suggest that critical pedagogy and popular culture form a powerful combination that allow students to draw upon their personal experiences to better learn the literacy skills needed to navigate the literacies of power associated with schooling while also learning the language and literacy skills needed to deconstruct schooling and society. This is particularly important for those students who find themselves disempowered within dominant institutions such as the media or public schools.

Chapters 4 through 7 provide four case studies of critical pedagogy that used popular culture as a tool to develop academic literacy and critical language among adolescent students. I now want to turn from philosophy to psychology in order to conclude this chapter by discussing some possible connections between the teaching of popular culture and increases in student motivation.

Teaching Popular Culture Can Provide Greater Motivation for Many Students

There is a great deal that motivational psychology can say to literacy educators about the reasons that students may or may not be inclined to participate fully in classroom contexts and there is a correlation between achievement motivation and actual achievement. In this section, I will examine two prevalent theories of achievement motivation, *expectancy-value theories* and *social cognitive theories*, to consider how the teaching of popular culture may play a role in increasing students' motivation to achieve in school.

Expectancy-Value Models of Motivation

Eccles and Wigfield (Eccles, 1993; Eccles et al., 1989; Wigfield, 1994; Wigfield and Eccles, 1992, 2000) have developed a social cognitive model that focuses on students' expectations for academic success and their perceived value of academic tasks. This builds upon earlier work of Atkinson (1957, 1964) who developed a model of achievement motivation that highlighted the importance of motives, probability for success, and incentive value (Pintrich and Schunk, 2002).

Utilizing the expectancy-value model of achievement motivation, it is easy to understand how the use of popular culture in literacy classrooms could increase the motivation of students to achieve. When considering the first component of the Eccles and Wigfield model, one can argue to the degree that teachers are able to include elements of popular culture that are familiar to students, that students will have greater expectation for academic success. For example, in my classroom activities that involved popular music and film, I found that students possessed a great deal more confidence and expectation for success.

When considering the second component of the Eccles and Wigfield model, it is also easy to understand why students would have a greater incentive value to learn popular culture as opposed to other segments of the school curriculum. As I have shown earlier in this chapter, popular culture is thematically relevant to the lives of young people; and quantitatively, they value popular culture as evidenced by their dollars and hours of consumption. I have found that students have a greater incentive to learn about genres and texts that are immediately relevant to their everyday lives. Further, I have found that allowing students some ownership over the selection process increases expectation for success and incentive to participate, though I argue in chapter 8 that final decisions about popular cultural content need to reside with the teacher.

Social Cognitive Theory

Bandura (1986, 1997) the most notable proponent of social cognitive theory, postulates that, by observing models, people learn skills and strategies that they use when they are motivated to do so and the situation seems appropriate . Some core concepts of Bandura's theory include enactive learning, learning by doing, and vicarious learning, which occurs in the absence of overt performance, but involves observing models that are live, symbolic, electronic, or in print (Pintrich and Schunk, 2002). Further, Bandura felt that *self-efficacy*, or one's perceived capabilities to learn or perform actions at a designated level, to be a key factor in achievement motivation.

The examples I present in this book demonstrate that teaching popular culture enables the preconditions for achievement motivation as laid out in social cognitive theory. Elsewhere (Morrell, 2002), I have argued that film viewings and discussions are uniquely social situations in literacy classrooms that can lead to the creation of viable learning communities. Whereas reading is generally an individual activity at the secondary level, film watching, whether in a theater or a classroom, is a social activity in a shared physical space.

The social nature of film and television watching allows for extensive peer and teacher modeling in the classroom. The students, for instance, are able to see how different viewers posture themselves, how people pay attention, and how astute viewers react to various scenes and images. In my classes, the students were able to see when I or one of their peers thought a scene or image was important enough to annotate in our notes. More than once, a student would ask that the film be stopped if several students or the teacher were taking notes for a reason that she or he did not understand. These breaks would open up space for dialogue on critical content, as well as conversations about how to take notes on a film. There would be times when the students were watching a film or listening to music when I would ask them to compare notes to see how different individuals make sense of a similar text.

Another important component of teaching popular culture involves the creation of opportunities for enactive and vicarious learning. I have found it important not only to have opportunities for students to learn by doing, but to learn by doing together. Collaborative learning communities actually can allow for simultaneous enactive and vicarious learning as students have opportunities to do and watch within the same activity.

Throughout the units described in chapters 4 through 7, these activities took on various forms including preparing presentations for peers, conducting independent research, creating a magazine, or reaching out to younger children in the community. Like Bandura, I feel that these social learning environments help the self-efficacy and, ultimately, the individual achievement motivation of students.

In this chapter, I have attempted to articulate a foundation for the teaching of popular culture that includes literacy theory, cultural studies, critical theory, and motivational psychology. Now that the foundation has been laid, the next four chapters move forward to the presentation and discussion of actual examples of the practice of teaching popular culture, specifically focusing on the teaching of film, music, media studies, and sports. Hopefully, these concrete examples can serve the dual purpose of adding relevant context to the conceptual foundation that has been laid over the first three chapters, while also stimulating generative internal and external conversations about the potential for utilizing popular culture to promote literacy development in ways not mentioned in this text.

Part Two
The Practice

Chapter 4

Teaching
Popular Music

Vignettes From Practice

Vignette #1

A group of four high school students enter the Student Union build-ing at a nearby university. Wanda and Camille are carrying their notebooks. Charles trails behind with the digital video camera. Fran-cisco stays close to Charles as the two will switch off with the filming. Once they have refined their questions and gained confidence, they begin approaching the college students who are eating lunch, shop-ping, or hanging out. Wanda explains to potential interviewees that she and her colleagues are conducting research relating to the impact of hip-hop culture on the lives of youth. Most of the college students are willing to participate and the group collects a multitude of data to use in their report.

Vignette #2

It has been several minutes since the bell rang releasing students for break, yet the classroom is still crowded with students who are

cont.

discussing the most recent group presentation from the Poet in Society unit. The specific topic of debate is an interpretation that V offered of a line from a Goodie Mob song which states, "Look out for the man with the mask on the white pony." V and her classmates argue back and forth over whether the man and his horse represent the government, corporate America, or whether he represents racism in general. References are made to former CIA agent William Cooper's Behold a Pale Horse, *which chronicles government conspiracies and cover-ups. The end of break finds these students still defending their respective interpretations until they are sent off to their third period classes.*

Popular Music in the Lives of America's Youth

There is no doubt that popular music plays a preeminent role in the lives of America's youth. One need look no further than the amazing success of MTV or the sheer number of CDs that are sold to young people annually. Popular music also has a clear and prominent impact on fashion, hairstyles, youth language, and youth attitudes toward authority and dominant institutions. This chapter makes the legitimate case that, for today's youth, hip-hop is the popular music. It is a genre whose popularity transcends race, class, and gender. In a 1999 *Time* magazine article entitled "Hip-hop Nation," it was reported that more people purchase hip-hop CDs than any other genre of music in any time in history. Further, though the music and culture are frequently associated with urban America and with youth of color, more than 70% of hip-hop CDs are purchased by white middle-class teens. Hip-hop is a genre whose motifs of oppression and resistance resonate with a large national and increasingly international audience. For this reason, I have focused in this chapter on the teaching of hip-hop culture, though these examples could easily be changed or expanded to include any other genre of popular music. In the conclusion, I talk more about strategies for incorporating other forms of popular music.

This chapter lays out the history and background of hip-hop music and culture, explaining its origins in urban, post-industrial America. It also explains how hip-hop music has gained importance as a counter-cultural voice of resistance even as it has become co-opted by mainstream, corporate interests. The heart of the chapter presents and analyzes an intervention that used hip-hop as a bridge to canonical poetry in an urban secondary English classroom. I explain the rationale for the unit, the various goals and objectives, the class activities, and share classroom vignettes, samples of student dialogue and student work, and excerpts from interviews conducted with students at the unit's conclusion. I also examine a research project in which a team of high school students from the South Bay Project investigate the impact of hip-hop culture on youth in America. I describe the project, its context as part of a larger seminar on youth research, and present examples of the students in action along with excerpts from their final presentation and report.

As an English teacher at North Bay High, I witnessed the impact of hip-hop music and culture on all of my students. I saw at the same time that the culture's influence seemed to transcend race as students from a variety of ethnic backgrounds were strongly influenced by the culture (Mahiri, 1998). At the same time, through looking at the literacy practices (Barton and Hamilton, 2000) associated with engagement with hip-hop, I also saw that students, in this non-mainstream cultural practice (Ferdman, 1990) were exhibiting the critical and analytical skills that we wanted them to bring to academic texts from the canon. I ultimately decided that I could utilize hip-hop music and culture to forge a common and critical discourse that was centered upon the lives of the students, yet transcended the racial divide, and allowed me to tap into students' lives in ways that promoted academic literacy and critical consciousness.

Baker (1993), Farley (1999), and George (1999) all argue that the creative people who are talking about youth culture in a way that makes sense happen to be rappers, and the youth are responding in many ways. Hip-hop artists sold more than 81 million CDs, tapes, and albums in 1998, more than any other genre of music. Taking their cue from the music industry, other major corporations are creating advertising schemes that cater to the "hip-hop generation." Even mainstream Hollywood, with films such as Warren Beatty's *Bulworth*, has dealt with issues related to hip-hop. Although the music is largely criticized by politicians, religious groups, and some women's groups, its proponents claim that it is here to stay as it represents a resistant voice of today's youth through its articulation of problems that the young people of this generation and all Americans face on a daily basis.

Rose (1994) and Tabb Powell (1991) argue strongly that hip-hop music is the representative voice of urban youth as the genre was created by and for urban youth. Tabb Powell states:

[Rap] emerged from the streets of inner-city neighborhoods as a genuine reflection of the hopes, concerns, and aspirations of urban Black youth in this, the last quarter of the 20th century. Rap is essentially a homemade, street-level musical genre . . . Rap lyrics concentrate primarily on the contemporary African American experience. . . . Every issue within the Black community is subject to exposition in the rap arena. Hit rap tunes have broached touchy subjects such as sex, sexism, racism, and crime. . . . Rap artists, they contend, "don't talk that love stuff, but [rather] educate the listeners." (p. 245)

Many rappers consider themselves educators and see at least a portion of their mission as promoting consciousness within their communities (Lipsitz, 1994; Rose, 1994). As articulated by Freire, the raising of critical consciousness in people who have been oppressed is a first step in helping them to obtain critical literacy and, ultimately, liberation from oppressive ideologies. The influence of rap as a voice of resistance and liberation for urban youth proliferates through such artists as Lauryn Hill, Pras, and Wyclef Jean of the Refugee Camp, Public Enemy, Nas, and Mos Def who endeavor to bring an accurate, yet critical depiction of the urban situation to a hip-hop generation.

I further argue that hip-hop texts are literary texts and can be used to scaffold literary terms and concepts and ultimately foster literary interpretations. Hip-hop texts are rich in imagery and metaphor and can be used to teach irony, tone, diction, and point of view. Hip-hop texts can also be analyzed for theme, motif, plot, and character development. It is very possible to perform feminist, Marxist, structuralist, psychoanalytic, or postmodernist critiques of particular hip-hop texts, the genre as a whole, or sub-genres such as "gangsta rap." Once learned, these analytic and interpretative tools developed through engagement with popular cultural texts can be applied to canonical texts as well (Lee, 1992). If one goal of critical educators is to empower urban students to analyze complex literary texts, hip-hop texts can be used as a bridge linking the seemingly vast span between the streets and the world of academics.

Hip-hop texts, given their thematic nature, can be equally valuable as springboards for critical discussions about contemporary issues facing today's youth. Provocative rap texts can be brought into the classrooms and discussion topics may be produced from a listening/reading of the text. These discussions may lead to more thoughtful analyses that could translate into expository writing, the production of poetic texts or a commitment to social action for community empowerment.

Teaching hip-hop as a music and culture of resistance can facilitate the development of critical consciousness in all youth. Analyzing the critical social commentary produced by the Refugee Camp, Public Enemy, or Nas may lead to conscious-raising discussions, essays, and research projects attempting to locate an explanation for the current state of affairs for adolescents today. The knowledge reflected in these lyrics could engender discussions of esteem, power, place, and purpose or encourage students to further their own knowledge of urban sociology and politics. In this way, hip-hop music should stand on its own merit in the academy and be a worthy subject of study in its own right rather than necessarily leading to something more "acceptable" like a Shakespeare text. It can, however, serve as a bridge between urban cultures and the literary canon.

Given the social, cultural, and academic relevance of hip-hop music and culture, a colleague and I (Morrell and Duncan-Andrade, 2002) designed a classroom unit with three objectives:

1. To utilize our students' involvement with hip-hop culture to scaffold the critical and analytical skills that they already possess.

2. To provide students with the awareness and confidence they need to transfer these skills into/onto the literary texts from the canon.

3. To enable students to critique the messages sent to them through the popular cultural media that permeate their everyday lives.

The unit was designed to incorporate hip-hop music into a "traditional" senior English poetry unit. Our desires were to increase motivation and participation in discussions and assignments, and to teach critical essay writing and literary terminology in the context of, among other types of poetry, rap music. We also wanted to situate hip-hop historically and socially and discuss its inception as a response to urban post-industrialism. Further, we wished to encourage youth to view elements of popular culture through a critical lens and to critique messages sent to them through popular media and to help students understand the intellectual integrity, literary merit, and social critique contained within elements of their own youth culture.

There were several goals and objectives for this unit that combined our simultaneous agendas of tapping into popular culture and facilitating academic and critical literacy development. To accomplish this, we needed to cover the poetry of the Elizabethan age, the Puritan Revolution, and the Romantics, which were a part of the district-mandated curriculum for 12th grade English and which they would be expected to have knowledge of for the Advanced Placement exam and college English. It was also important to learn about the poets in the context of the literary and historical periods in which they wrote to gain a greater understanding of the role poetry plays as a critique of its contemporary society.

In addition to a critical exposure to the literary canon, we felt it important to concentrate on the development of issues and ideas presented in poetry and song as a vehicle to expository writing. Our objectives were

- To develop oral and written debate skills;
- To facilitate the ability to work in groups;
- To help students to deliver formal public presentations;
- To teach students how to critique a poem/song in a critical essay;
- To help students to develop note-taking skills in lectures and presentations; and
- To help students to become comfortable writing in different poetic forms such as the sonnet, elegy, and ballad

We began the unit with an overview of poetry in general attempting to redefine poetry and the role of a poet in society. We emphasized the importance of understanding the historical period in which a poem was written to come to a deep interpretation of the poem. In the introductory lecture, we outlined all of the historical/literary periods that would be covered in the unit (Elizabethan, Puritan Revolution, Romantics, and Metaphysical poets from England, and the Civil War, Harlem Renaissance, Civil Rights Movement, and Post Industrial Revolution in the United States). It was our intention to place hip-hop music—as a post-industrial art form—along side these other historical periods and poems so that the students would be able to use a period and genre of poetry they were familiar with as a lens with which to examine the other literary works and also to encourage the students to re-evaluate the manner in which they view elements of their popular culture.

The second major portion of the unit involved a group presentation of a canonical poem along with a hip-hop text. The groups were commissioned to prepare a justifiable interpretation of their texts situating each within its specific historical and literary period, while also analyzing the link between the two. There were eight groups for this portion who were, after a week of preparation, each given a class period to present to the class and have their arguments critiqued by their peers. The groups were assigned as illustrated in Table 4.1.

Table 4.1*		
Group	Poem	Song
1	"Kubla Khan," Coleridge	"If I Ruled the World," Nas
2	"Love Song of J. Alfred Prufrock," Eliot	"The Message," Grand Master Flash
3	"O Me! O Life!," Whitman	"Don't Believe the Hype," Public Enemy
4	"Immigrants in Our Own Land," Baca	"The World Is a Ghetto," Geto Boys
5	"Sonnet 29," Shakespeare	"Affirmative Action," Nas
6	"The Canonization," Donne	"Manifest," Refugee Camp
7	"Repulse Bay," Chin	"Good Day," Ice Cube
8	"Still I Rise," Angelou	"Cell Therapy," Goodie Mob

*Other poems used for this unit were "Let America Be America Again" by Langston Hughes and "Elegy Written in a Country Churchyard" by Thomas Gray.

In addition to the group presentations, students were asked to complete an anthology of ten poems that contained an elegy, a ballad, a sonnet, and a poem that described a place with which they were familiar. The title of the poem was to be the place that was featured. The students were also asked to write a poem that conveyed a mood, a poem that dealt with a political, social, or economic problem that was important to them (i.e., racism, teen pregnancy, drug abuse, police brutality, poverty, homelessness, and so forth), a love poem, a poem that celebrated a particular facet of life (such as first date, summertime, graduation), and two open poems that dealt with whatever subject students wanted and written in any style they desired. Following the group presentations, we held a poetry reading where each student selected five of his/her original poems to read for the class giving brief comments on each poem such as the context or a special meaning. For the outside of class assignment, students were allowed to pick any song of their choice and write a five to seven page critical essay of that song. They were also required to submit a transcription of that song.

The unit held consistent with the original goals of being culturally and socially relevant, critically exposing students to the literary canon, and facilitating the development of college-level expository writing. The positioning of hip-hop as a genre of poetry written largely in response to post-industrialism was a concept with which the students were able to relate. The issues of joblessness, poverty, rage, and alienation all had resonance to the urban youth culture of which the students were all a part. The foregrounding of hip-hop as a genre of poetry also helped to facilitate the transition to understanding the role individual poets may have played in their own societies.

The students were able to generate some excellent interpretations as well as make interesting links between the canonical poems and the rap texts. For instance, one group articulated that both Grand Master Flash and T. S. Eliot gazed out into their rapidly deteriorating societies and saw a "wasteland." Both poets were essentially apocalyptic in nature as they witnessed death, disease, and decay. Both poems also talk about a message, indicating the role of a poet in society as a messenger or prophet. Another group discussed the role of allegory in their two texts in which both John Donne and the artists from the Refugee Camp utilize relationships with lovers to symbolize the love and agony poets can feel for their societies.

The unit was consistent with the basic tenets of critical pedagogy in that it was situated in the experiences of the students (as opposed to those of the teacher), called for critical dialogue, a critical engagement of the text, and related the texts to larger social and political issues. The students were not only engaged and able to use this expertise and positionality as subjects of the post-industrial world to make powerful connections to canonical texts, they were also able to have fun learning about a culture and a genre of music with which they had great familiarity. Ultimately, our experiences introducing hip-hop and other elements of popular culture into traditional curricula lead us to believe that there are countless possibilities for literacy educators who wish to jump outside of the box and tap into the worlds of their students in order to make more powerful connections with traditional academic texts and to affirm, in meaningful ways, the everyday lives of their students.

The Hip-Hop Research Project

In partnership with the South Bay Unified School District, a major research university offered an introductory summer seminar for South Bay High school students in the field of the sociology of education, ED 001—Special Topics in Sociology of Education. The seminar invited a group of working-class Latino and African American youth to read seminal works in sociology of education and participate in a set of mini-research projects around the broad theme of "Race, Class, and Access in American Education." While all of the student participants had recently completed 10th grade at a local high school, they represented a fairly broad range of academic backgrounds. Over the course of three intensive weeks of study, the high school students worked in five-member teams to produce a piece of original research that they presented to a panel of university faculty members with expertise in the area of educational sociology.

One research group in particular studied the impact of hip-hop music and culture on high school students in America and the implications of this impact on how teachers approach the standardized curriculum. This group created and disseminated a survey to high school students and conducted interviews with teachers, friends and family, and undergraduates at a nearby university. During the three weeks of the seminar, student participants spent an hour with the whole group and two hours in the small groups with their research team advisor which, in this case, happened to be me. During the two-hour research team meetings, the students discussed concepts and readings relating to the sociology of education, learned the various aspects of the research process, prepared interview protocols and surveys, analyzed transcripts, and prepared presentations of their findings. On the final day of the seminar, the students presented their work to a group of university faculty involved in research relating to the sociology of education, parents, and other interested parties.

The summer seminar sought to place high school students in the role of *legitimate peripheral participants* within the broader community of practice of sociology of education research focused on the theme of access and equity (Lave and Wenger, 1991). Lave and Wenger define legitimate peripheral participation as an approach to learning and membership in which beginners have full access to full membership within a community without having full responsibility for membership. That is, the community establishes a process of changing participation over time that will result in becoming full participants. According to two educational sociologists that were interviewed, becoming a full participant in the field entailed developing competence in the literature, the research process, and the important issues. Novices in educational sociology (usually advanced undergraduates or graduate students) begin to demonstrate competence in several ways. They recognize critical questions in the field and identify answerable questions. They also demonstrate an understanding of difficult concepts by applying them to everyday situations.

Students in the summer seminar manifested emerging competence along these lines throughout the course of their research. Importantly, these demonstrations of competence arose in the process of being inducted into the research university's community of practice. The seminar students' participation changed over the course of the seminar on three levels—each of which speaks to their induction into the broader community of practice as well as their emerging "readiness." First, they appropriated the tools and culture of the research community. I mean by this that the students understood and internalized the language, culture, and purpose of research as they synthesized existing literature and ideas with their own burgeoning research projects. Second, students took on new identities through these new forms of participation. They began to see themselves not merely as passive objects but as participants, questioners, and investigators with something to contribute to the world of ideas. Third, they asserted more of a sense of ownership and control over the entire practice. Students in the seminar presentations commanded the center of attention in assuming the authority of research "experts" who were able to present findings, make recommendations, evaluate the viability of research alternatives, and set agendas for follow-up research.

The Presentation of the Hip-Hop Project

On the day of the final presentations, the project occupied a room reserved for special meetings and presentations. Called the Reading Room, it is adorned with tall solid oak bookshelves that contain bound volumes of scholarly writings from journals and other distinguished literature. Also in the room are two long oak tables that are often put together during meetings to make the room more cozy, a lectern, and fluffy recliner-type chairs that are usually situated in the nooks between bookshelves but, for now, are placed in the back of the room behind several rows of "convention" seats. One oak table sits in front of the rows. On the table sit three binders containing a program of the presentation, the summer seminar readers, and proposals for the various research projects. There are also copies of the "Hip-Hop Project," a paper completed by the hip-hop group, and copies of the PowerPoint presentations from the language, family, and resistance groups. Behind the great oak table are three tall wooden chairs reserved for the professors who are the distinguished guests of the presentation. All three professors are located in the school of education and their research on students of color and urban education is nationally renowned. Behind the professors are some forty chairs filled with friends and family of students, officials from the students' home school district, university faculty and staff, and a group of ACLU attorneys and their (student) clients that the resistance team had interviewed.

There is a general buzz throughout the room as groups and advisors huddle together, plan last-minute strategies and situate the room to their liking. Between setting up and greeting early arrivals with programs and papers, the advisors try to offer words of encouragement to students as they continue to pace and rehearse. Charles wants to go over the methodology section one more time so he approaches his advisor in the front of the room to make sure that his talk is fine. He is also worried because Wanda, another member of his group, is a few minutes late and audience members are already beginning to arrive. I assure him that Wanda will show up and tell him not to worry.

In the hip-hop group presentation, Camille begins by introducing the group as Tanya retrieves her posters that are displayed around the room. Charles and Francisco stand behind Camille.

Camille: Our group is researching hip-hop music and its impact on teens and how it can be used in the school's curriculum.

The problem that our research project addresses is the inequality that is promoted through the school's curriculum. The inequality is manifested through the fact that not everybody has a fair shot and that there is unequal achievement. The ways that inequalities are promoted through the curriculum are: (1) It justifies oppression and (2) Different people's cultures are excluded from the school's curriculum. Our research is important, because by studying hip-hop culture, people can learn about their own experiences so that they can become critical of the world.

Camille has a schema for the research process of a question stemming from a problem and inspiring a study that seeks to find answers or provide further explanation of that problem.

Charles: Our research question is what is the impact of hip-hop culture on high school students in urban America and our research group came up with a definition of hip-hop culture. It's urban Americans expressing their struggles in Urban America where they are forced to deal with poverty and alienation. This expression occurs through rap, R&B, and language, and how they dress and their attitude toward authority and society.

Charles and Wanda have developed this definition of hip-hop culture themselves and take great pride in predicating the research upon a culture that they have had the power to define.

During his discussion of methodology, Charles refers to the hip-hop cohort not as a group, but as a research team. These are his classmates from high school yet, in this arena, they are working together on an ambitious three-week research agenda. This language usage points to the ability of the new space to create room for new identities and allows Charles to see himself and his peers in a different light.

Charles: To find a solution to our research problem, each member of our research team took pictures of things in our community that represent hip-hop. We also interviewed teachers that were here in a summer institute. We also distributed 24 surveys to high school students that were here for a technology program. We also walked around the university campus with a video camera, and we had questions that we asked like did they think that hip-hop had a big impact on our youth and some of them were like kinda camera shy and they would agree to answer our questions, but when they saw the camera they were like, they got scared off and wouldn't answer our questions. But I don't understand how teachers . . . teachers say students of color never do anything positive, but when we do something positive, they don't help us out.

Throughout the hip-hop group's presentation, my sole task is to switch the overheads. The students are in control here. They are actually the instructors at this point. They have legitimate sociological knowledge to impart about the intersection of reproduction theory, critical pedagogy, and hip-hop music. They have control of the mechanical tools of research such as the overheads and posters, but they are also able to navigate the discourse and terminology of qualitative research, which they employ to serve their purposes. At this point, these young students are the experts at where this theory intersects with practice. This process also has amazing consequences for the students' development of academic literacy skills. They learn how to conduct and transcribe interviews, how to analyze survey data, and write a professional-quality report that was disseminated to university faculty and graduate students. For the remainder of their high school tenure, these students would continue to reference and push upon the hip-hop research that started in this seminar. For example, Wanda was one of several students who presented the hip-hop research to the English department at South Bay High. She, Camille, and Charles all presented this research to a statewide literacy organization. Some of the teachers these students addressed decided to incorporate hip-hop culture and music into their English curricula as a direct result of the powerful presentation.

Considerations When Teaching Popular Music

Given that popular music changes so rapidly and that there are so many popular songs at any given time, the task of making appropriate musical selections can be daunting for English teachers. By contrast, there are only a handful of films that teachers would have to consider in a given year compared with hundreds of songs. There are, of course magazines (see Appendix J) and shows such as MTV's "Total Request Live" that crown the song and the star of the moment. There are also the icons that transcend particular moments that teachers will have no trouble identifying. On the other hand, there are important lesser-known and underground musicians to consider. One may ask whether these musicians are even popular if they are not widely known. Based on the criteria I offered in chapter 2, I can say that artists definitely can be considered popular and worthy of study even if they are relatively obscure within the mainstream media.

Certainly, teachers should consult with their students early and often about the artists, songs, and genres that have had and are having a big impact on their lives. But this does not let teachers off the hook. Teachers must understand that, although all of their students listen to music, they are not all equally tapped into the popular culture. Teachers need to find informants—students who are intimately connected to multiple genres of popular music and can give them the expert advice they require. These are the students who play in bands, are president of the hip-hop society, or write lyrics in little notebooks that they carry everywhere. These students can prove invaluable in identifying trends, spotting visionaries, providing a detailed history of a particular genre, and locating hard to find music. They can also help with the processes of decoding, translating, and interpreting, though the teacher must ultimately find her own way. In my experience, these closet artists and musicians have been happy to play this role.

Teachers also have a responsibility to highlight themes and generate topics for opening and facilitating discussions. They can also work collaboratively with students to create assignments and rubrics that simultaneously honor students' interests, while providing access to relevant academic skills. Sharing ownership of the classroom space and incorporating popular culture does not mean letting go or adopting a hands-off policy. Teachers definitely need to keep their hands on; it is still their class. Students need them to help illuminate the bigger picture, to monitor the classroom space, and to make explicit the connections between students' strengths and literacies and cultures of power (Delpit, 1988). Sometimes this means saying no to particular texts or selecting songs that may not have the largest appeal, but are important for the larger goals of the class. It certainly means working diligently to develop a sophisticated understanding of popular music and maintaining an affirming, yet critical, stance toward popular texts that enables them to challenge students in their beliefs and interpretations.

It has been said other places in this book, but it bears repeatings that the "how" of teaching popular culture is just as important as the "what." Simply inserting popular selections into a teacher-dominated classroom will not change outcomes. The effective teaching of popular music must occur in a dialogic space that acknowledges student voice and encourages student action. Students must be given permission to engage popular music in ways that respect them as critical cultural consumers as opposed to ignorant partakers of a base and common culture. Critical teachers of popular music will find ways to simultaneously affirm and challenge while maintaining a problem-posing environment in which students feel free to challenge each other and the teacher as well. These teachers will also create spaces that enable students to come to their own readings of musical texts while learning from the readings of their peers, and trying on critical lenses that force them to read from marginalized positions.

Teachers should feel confident using popular music in conjunction with poetry, by itself, as part of theme-based, multi-genre units or as part of larger research on youth and popular culture. The possibilities are virtually endless for the teacher who wants to bring popular music into her or his English classroom.

Chapter 5

Teaching Film and Television

Vignette From Practice

The class is viewing The Godfather. The lights are on. Having watched several other films together, they are familiar with the routine. As I survey the classroom, I see that there is near complete engagement; everyone has a writing instrument and a notebook. As is the case with the opening scene, we stop frequently to discuss the moves of the director and the actors. Who is hidden in the shadows? Who is captured in full light? To whom does the camera defer? Who does the camera subordinate? Who speaks? Who gets spoken to? What images are highlighted? How are religious images portrayed? What requires close-ups? Long shots? What is the content and nature of the musical score? What other elements of sound are essential? How are the women positioned in relation to the men? Who has the power? Who wants it?

By the end of the first few scenes, we have developed hypotheses and identified themes that we will revisit throughout the viewing of the trilogy. As is normally the case, the students are engaged and have much to contribute to this opening dialogue. Taking in the passionate comments, the intense gazes, and the furious scribbling of notes; and always seeing something new, or learning from a student comment or question, I am reminded how truly extraordinary a piece filmmaking is The Godfather trilogy.

Film and Television in the Lives of America's Youth

There is no doubt that adolescents watch a great deal of television and film. Quantitative media studies and Neilsen ratings, for instance, tell us that young people, like their parents, spend more of their waking hours watching television than any other activity. Traditionally, secondary English teachers have denounced engagements with these media as negative influences on the academic literacy development of their students. During my own days as a student, I remember the simplistic comparisons between watching television or film and reading books with the former cast as wastes of time and resource and the latter tied to academic skills development. Nowhere was this attitude more prevalent than in school where, in my experience, television shows and films were reserved for substitute teachers, lazy Fridays, or the week after standardized tests. Film and television were treated as rewards or fillers and not as opportunities to learn.

Fortunately, the fate of film in English courses is improving, at least at the postsecondary level. In colleges and universities all over the nation and the world, film is treated as a complex and intellectual media worthy of academic study (Scholes, 1998). Many of the elite English programs now offer critical film studies courses and concentrations. Scholarly magazines feature film commentary and a host of new books are written each year that apply critical lenses to the study of film. I argue in this chapter that secondary English teachers can borrow from their postsecondary peers as I explore the potential of teaching film in secondary English classrooms to make meaningful connections between the everyday literacy practices of diverse teens and the academic literacies of school. I begin with an explanation of several classroom units that I created which juxtaposed film texts with canonical literary texts. Next, I briefly discuss my work with pre-service and practicing teachers and conclude by offering suggestions to those English teachers who are considering incorporating more popular film into their curricula.

Lessons From the Field

I designed several units that combined a major film with a canonical text of similar themes. The first unit analyzed for this chapter juxtaposes *The Godfather* trilogy against Homer's *The Odyssey*. The second unit joins Richard Wright's *Native Son* with the film *A Time to Kill*. In creating and evaluating the units I started with two basic goals:

1. To analyze the viability of utilizing popular culture to scaffold the issues and cultures that are relevant to urban youth in order to promote the development of critical and analytical skills that can be used to interpret texts from the literary canon.

2. To assess the potential for providing students with activities and techniques that would facilitate a transfer of these skills from popular cultural texts into/onto the literary and academic texts from the canon.

Only after watching the culmination of the units and making sense of the academic and social outcomes did I add this third research goal.

3. To determine the capacity of this approach to enable students to critique the messages sent to them through the literary canon as well as the societal institutions that permeate their lives such as the popular cultural media and urban schooling.

Ultimately, I developed several units in which students critically investigated television and film in my classes. Viewing, however, did not occur with the lights out for fifty-five minutes between bells. Students watched the films with the lights on for 20–25 minutes and spent the latter portion of each period in close analysis of the text, often proceeding scene by scene and discussing plot, character, and theme as well as the visual images that the director used to make her or his point. The students were required to take notes and would frequently ask to freeze a frame or to go back to review a scene where there were some questions. It was also not uncommon for students to differ in their interpretations and have heated discussions over possible meanings of images, camera angles, dialogue, and so on. In one classroom unit, we watched the entire *Godfather* trilogy while discussing epic film and literature and the American Dream. At the culmination of the unit, the students held a debate over whether Michael Corleone, the protagonist, portrayed an epic hero. In their preparation for this debate, students were able to revisit their notes and point to specific images and scenes to make their respective cases. During their final exam, these students were asked to discuss, through the characters of Kay, Connie, and Mrs. Corleone, the role and treatment of women in this epic piece (see Appendixes C and D).

I present several ethnographic narratives (Berg, 2001) each chosen to represent a particular stage of the unit. Each narrative is illustrative of the powerful connections that students were able to make between the popular cultural text, the canonical text, and their everyday lives. The narratives are arranged chronologically according to the order in which they occur in the units. Although two distinct units are discussed in this chapter with the *Odyssey/Godfather* unit preceding *Native Son/A Time to Kill*, both units adhered to the same structure of film watching, book discussion, and preparing for and delivering classroom presentations. The first narrative occurs during a film-watching section of *A Time to Kill*. The second narrative follows a group preparing for a presentation on *The Odyssey* and *The Godfather*. The third narrative documents a presentation on *The Odyssey* and *The Godfather*. The final narrative relates an episode that occurred on the final day of the unit while a student group addresses the question of whether justice prevailed for Carl Lee Hailey in *A Time to Kill* and Bigger Thomas in *Native Son*.

Free Carl Lee

The class is watching *A Time to Kill* and, during this particular segment, there are racial riots around the trial of Carl Lee. Carl Lee Hailey is a black man who is on trial for killing the two white men who raped his daughter and left her for dead and, as the trial approaches in the film, racial tensions escalate. The NAACP comes from "up North" to lobby on the side of Carl Lee and the KKK comes from the Deep South to lobby on the side of the two white men that were killed.

As the racial tensions escalate in the movie, the class becomes more emotionally charged and begins to identify with the African Americans in the film and actually root for them. There is one portion during a racial riot where an African American woman and a Klan member are having an argument and they end up getting into a fistfight that emerges into a race riot. As the African American woman hits the man, Shalia jumps out of her seat and claps her hands and says, "Oh, I like that one." Also, as the riot begins to escalate on the film, Claude, another student in the class is leaning forward in his seat and looks as if he's more attentive and he starts laughing and clapping. Lu and Chan who are sitting in the front also lean forward and Lu, picks up her pen and begins writing notes in preparation for the post-film discussion. Then in the film one of the young black boys torches a Klan member; actually it is Stump Sisson who is the Grand Wizard of the Klan. He gets killed during this scene and I stopped the tape for a brief moment and asked, "Is this justice?" Shalia responds, "A little bit," and Robin, another student in the class replies, "On one side, one side has justice," while Alex, another African American student sitting in the back of the class is smiling and nodding his head in assent.

As the scene continues, Shalia turns around and asks a question of Claude, who is laughing and clapping his hands in approval. Alex comments on the police officer, Deputy Hastings, that is secretly with the Klan. "Isn't he a part of them?" he asks. Chan also interjects a comment to the group, so as the scene escalates, the attention in the class also escalates as students begin identifying and discussing with one another and actually becoming emotionally involved with the scene as they begin to simultaneously analyze the text and relate it to their own everyday experiences. As the section continues, the National Guard is called and Jake Brigance, the protagonist, has his house burned down by the Klan. Harry Rex, who is another white attorney, encourages Jake to drop the case. When that happens, Shalia responds that Harry Rex is making her "heck-a mad" for asking Jake to drop the case. It is as if Carl Lee Hailey and these characters are real to the class at this point. Jake turns down Harry Rex's offer and says that he is going to trial.

The scene shifts to the next day outside of the courthouse where the trial is about to take place. The NAACP is chanting "Free Carl Lee" and the Klan is chanting "Fry Carl Lee." I turned off the video at this point so we could discuss the segment. Claude puts his head down and says, "Why do you have to stop the tape here?" which is his daily routine. Chan raises her fist and yells, "Free Carl Lee!" and members of the class laugh.

The class, here, is beginning to relate the popular cultural text to their everyday lives. They are also using this understanding to facilitate textual analysis as well as a critical engagement with the text. This is a film and the story is fictional·and the characters are fictional, but the emotion surrounding the issues of racism and justice where the students are upset with characters and clapping and cheering and pumping fists shows that the students are politicizing this film and relating it to similar issues in their own lives. This relevance, I argue, leads to a deeper understanding that, in turn, facilitates a deeper analysis of this text. During the discussion of the film on this particular day, students including Lu and Chan describe incidents where they were victims of racial violence. Chan's raising her fist at the end of the film also indicates that she is identifying with

Carl Lee and the issues of the film as she is formulating her analysis of this film, which also informs her reading of the world.

Freeing Carl Lee, for these students, is victory for the African Americans, who are the oppressed group in the film. As members of oppressed groups within society, this perspective informs the students' identification with and analysis of the text. Several of the students have claimed that the torching of Sisson is justice and any exoneration of Carl Lee's actions is a victory for the oppressed and the students clearly in this case identify with this oppressed group. Their willingness to identify with this text enables them to bridge their worlds with the film text and to embrace the text at a critical level. Rather than looking at Carl Lee and Jake and Ellen as fictional characters, they are looking at what they represent to their own lives in creating that universal plane of knowledge. As they begin to relate the characters to their own everyday lives, they juxtapose the text against their lives and bring their everyday life experiences into their critical interpretation of this text.

During the post-film discussion, I ask whether the black boy who killed the Klan wizard was guilty of murder. Robin and Chan nod their heads in assent while Shalia and Jessica claim that it was self-defense. Claude responds that the Klan has instigated the skirmish that leads to Sisson's death. "It's the way that they came to the courthouse," he contends. When I respond that an African American woman actually started the altercation by punching a white man, 10 students raise their hands to disagree, all speaking at once in unintelligible, yet emotionally packed chatter.

The point gets made that the guilt of African Americans and White Americans in the scene is not equivalent because the Whites have power, privilege, and a stake in the status quo while the African Americans in this scenario are largely reactionary. I offer that Stump Sisson was wrong and didn't deserve to die but, on the other hand, the boy who killed him wasn't necessarily guilty of first-degree murder, therefore confusing simplistic notions of right and wrong and setting the stage for future discussions and debates.

As we begin to discuss our impending reenactment of the Bigger Thomas court trial, the connection is made between Clanton, Mississippi, and the city where North Bay High is located. Tiet recalls a recent incident between African Americans and Latinos at the school where the police were called in to intervene. Lu tells a story about how two Asian-American friends of hers were victims of attacks by African Americans. Shalia asks for more details about the incident as the class listens attentively. Although we cannot agree on whether there can be a single conception of justice for all, the entire class agrees that what happened to Lu's friends was wrong.

There is evidence in this narrative both of textual analysis and of critical engagement with the text. During the film watching and the post-film discussion, the students analyze the plot, characters, setting, and themes. They question and interrogate the motives of particular characters and critique the social values that are articulated in the film. Further, they are able to relate specific events in the text to a larger discussion of justice in society. There was also evidence of critical engagement as the students were able to relate their textual critiques to larger issues of power and access in society.

Chan's Chat Group

It is the final day of preparation for group presentations on *The Odyssey* and *The Godfather*. Lu, Tiet, Hong, and Chan are attempting to figure out the order and design of their presentation. Hong is closely reading the text to determine who initiated the affair between Odysseus and Calypso. "Oh, she started it," Tiet laughs and initiates the following dialogue:

Chan: Do you think that females have control of the males? I think so. Do you think so? (Laughing) I think females control males with sex (whole group laughs).

Tiet: (gesturing to her shoulder) They wear a sexy little thing and he be all under control (more laughter).

Chan, here, segues from the textual discussion of Odysseus and Calypso to introduce her worldview of femininity and sex roles comparing Calypso, a fictional goddess, with females in general. Tiet's response also shows a contemporization of the issue presented in the text. Her references to teasing and lingerie are clearly not from ancient Greece, yet aid the group in their close reading of this segment of the text as they connect it to an issue that has some relevance to their worlds.

As the conversation turns to the presentation, Tiet informs Hong that she will guide the group into their argument about the status of females. "Yes," Chan responds, "you have a very important part, and (turning to Tiet) so do you." When the conversation shifts to whether Odysseus ever slept with Nausicaa, Chan initiates another conversation:

Chan: (leaning over her desk to Hong and whispering) Did Odysseus sleep with Nausicaa, too?

Hong: (Blank expression)

Lu: (turning to the teacher) Mr. Morrell, did Odysseus ever sleep with Nausicaa?

Morrell: No, but he probably wanted to (at this Tiet looks at Hong and laughs). Remember, when she found him by the shore, she was already in love with him. . . .

Lu: It was like love at first sight?

Morrell: Yeah, he didn't sleep with her because her father was around.

Chan: You know what's kind of funny, he kind of liked (Nausicaa) but he didn't sleep with her, but the person he didn't like . . . he slept with.

Hong: Isn't she young enough to be his daughter?

Morrell: Yeah (Chan laughs).

Lu: Ooh, that's sick!

Chan: That's how it was. . . . that's what I was trying to tell you. That's the old ways, the old values. In new values you might think it's sick but, in the old values, it wasn't. It comes from the past to the present (gesturing in a circular motion), you know, in a circle.

If Chan's role is as leader of this group who seems to be comfortable with the conversational style of group preparation, Hong's role is as the textual expert. Although she is not as vocal as the other members, Chan assures her that her role is "a very important one." Hong's task is to clarify and assist the other group members in understanding the literal text. It is she who informs Tiet, after confirming in the text, that Calypso initiates the affair with Odysseus; and it is to her that Chan directs the question of the nature of Odysseus' relationship with Nausicaa. It is only when Hong is unable to respond that the teacher is consulted

Immediately following my response, Hong and Chan, through their statements, problematize the motives and actions of the main character. The conversation elevates beyond a mere understanding of the canonical text, as these students are willing to offer a feminist critique of the values of the protagonist. These critiques of Odysseus are predicated upon Chan's initial comments about female sex roles where Calypso and Odysseus became representatives of females and males respectively. Lu is also using her own value system to critique Odysseus' actions when she calls him "sick." She has also clearly gone beyond a mere comprehension of the text in calling his behavior into question. Chan, in her role as leader and facilitator of this group, acknowledges Lu's critique but also cautions her against using her value system to judge too hastily. Chan recognizes the limitations of contemporizing an ancient text without paying attention to the values of the time period in which the text was written. Chan doesn't dismiss Lu's analysis, but she adds to it a historical critique that, from the standpoint of his society, Odysseus' actions may not be that out of place.

The group members' ability to clarify, assist, and critique each other while also problematizing the text using both their value system and world knowledge coupled with a historical awareness allowed for a high-level engagement and criticism of a difficult canonical text. Chan's leadership, sensitivity, and knowledge of when to use popular cultural knowledge (I think females control men with sex) and when to draw the line tremendously aided her group's effectiveness.

That's the Problem with Females Nowadays

After we finished *The Godfather* epic and were through the first sixteen books of *The Odyssey*, the class was divided into four groups and each group had a week to prepare a presentation on a four-book segment from *The Odyssey*. Group 1 had books 1–4, Group 2 had books 5–8, Group 3 had books 9–12, and Group 4 had books 13–16. Following the week of preparation, each group was given a class period to present. For the initial 25–30 minutes of the presentation the group was to discuss their books and talk about what happened, including a discussion of how that four-book segment dealt with major themes and issues that we had been discussing as part of the unit that carried over from *The Godfather*, such as: treatment of women, the role of religion, the characterization of an epic hero, the idea of a voyage to manhood, and other themes that were laid out over the course of the unit. After the 30-minute presentation, each group was required to facilitate a 15–20-minute discussion in which they had to be prepared to ask questions of the class and respond to the questions and comments of their peers. On the days that they weren't presenting, students were required to take presentation notes to critique other presentations. The first group was responsible for books 1–4 and, during their question and answer period, the conversation turned toward Penelope and Athena as representatives of females and questions arose, such as: Were they strong characters or did they do women any good or were they examples of the traditional subservient female?

Jasmine volunteered to answer first and discussed the role of women in this (Greek) society at this time:

Jasmine: Even Athena, a goddess had to ask [a male deity] permission to help a mortal so someone who is already a mortal, Penelope, would have no chance against the suitors because they're men. They wouldn't even listen to Telemachus who was a man. . . . so, for her to ask them to leave wouldn't do any good.

Shalia: Shouldn't she at least make the suitors aware of her displeasure, that she was unhappy with them being at her house?

At this point, several students wanted to participate from the audience and Jessica began "correcting" Shalia on her critique of Penelope and Telemachus saying that Telemachus only became powerful to the extent that he became a man. Phong, a young man who sits in the back of class and rarely speaks raised his hand, but was beat to the punch by Lu, a gregarious and talkative young woman who sits in the front of the class who, at this point, just starts speaking and raises her hand mid-sentence:

Lu: I think that if Penelope had not led the suitors on then maybe they would have gotten a clue and left or did something. (By the time Lu had finished her comment three hands were raised, Natasha, Chan, and Phong. Phong was given the floor to speak.)

Phong: What I think is that the country (Ithaca) needed a king to lead them. They cannot wait for Odysseus to return because he might not come back. Somebody has to take over.

Lien: If it was so important for the country to have a leader they could have picked one instead of destroying Penelope's house and her life. That's no excuse to come into her home!

Shalia: If a suitor really wanted to marry Penelope then he could have gone to her father to ask permission rather than destroy Odysseus' and Penelope's house. Back in those days, you were supposed to go through the father to ask a lady's hand in marriage.

Chan: You can't blame her, she had no choice, that was the female's role (turning her comments to Phong). Also, if you don't know that Odysseus is dead, how can you go around and say, "Imma pick this king or that king?" It's not that simple (returning to the group); Penelope is a female and she has no rights.

Shalia: Does that make it right? Just because she's a female, she shouldn't have any rights?

Chan: I'm not talking about right now. I'm talking about in the past.

Shalia: No, in the past. Did it make it right then?

Chan: In our day, you can tell the suitor off, but in those days, the female can't say nothing. We can talk about Calypso and the other women, but it's all the same, females had no rights then.

Shalia: How do you think we got a voice in the modern day? It didn't just happen. It started back then. If it wasn't for someone in 1919 to speak out, we wouldn't have a voice now! Penelope, instead of sitting upstairs in her room weaving and crying, could have tried to say something then. It'd be better now. That's the problem with females nowadays. You think that you don't have a right and then you say that it's not right that we don't have a right to voice our opinions . . . even though things were bad "back then" it still took someone to stand up and change things or else "back then" would still be "right now."

Shalia and Chan have incorporated into the textual discussion a discussion of their present existence as females and members of oppressed groups. Both Shalia and Chan tap into their experiences as young women of color to critique the actions of Penelope, a fictional representation of women from a classical text.

Shalia: . . . and if it wasn't for someone to step up, it would still be like that now. If you just sit down now and say, "That's the way it was" and you're lax about that, anything that happens in your life right now, you're just going to say, "Oh that's the way it's supposed to be!"

Shalia has politicized the text, merging her critique of Penelope together with her own feminist politics. Penelope, in her opinion, is guilty of inaction and inaction will never lead to political change. According to Shalia, people who think like Penelope will always make excuses for the way things are and never attempt to make things better for themselves or for future generations. In justifying her stance, she makes the reference between the political climate in *The Odyssey* and the political climate for women historically utilizing the women's suffrage movement, all the way to the political climate today ending her critique with the statement, "that's the problem with females nowadays." Shalia, here, is not just tapping into her reservoir of historical knowledge of the women's suffrage movement and the Civil Right's movement to inform her interpretation of the text, but she is using the text to inform a discussion, a contemporary classroom discussion on the rights of women. Her statement, "that's the problem with females," is referring to Chan, who's in class, and also indirectly refers to Penelope and Athena, fictional characters created by a male poet, all on an equal plane. That you, Chan you, Penelope and you, Athena are all people that subordinate yourselves to the world or the majority at any given time. That complicit, non-revolutionary representation of the female, according to Shalia, will prevent females from ever being able to change things for themselves.

The Justice Connection

This is the final day of the second unit and the data collection for the research. Group 4 is presenting its findings on justice in *Native Son* and *A Time to Kill*. Phi begins by defining justice as fair and equal treatment. Given the existence of racism and sexism, Phi contends that justice can only be defined individually, not as a society. Because of the will of the majority, he argues, minorities will never receive justice in the United States.

Jasmine states that she believes the ones who receive justice are those with money and power, and those that do not receive justice are the poor and homeless. Referring to *Native Son,* she believes that the white community receives justice and that justice is denied to the black community. In *A Time to Kill,* Jasmine argues that Carl Lee Hailey never received justice "just because Jake and Carla went to their house with some nasty Peach Cobbler." Carl and his family still had to live with racism in the South, and he still had to "sleep at night with the image of the murders he committed and knowing that his daughter was raped and called out his name but he wasn't there to answer."

Viet dealt with the final question of what ultimate commentary the film and the novel make on justice in American society. Viet responds that justice means different things to different people and sometimes, as with Carl Lee, you have to take the law into your own hands to receive justice. Viet also believes that Bigger Thomas receives justice when he takes the law into his own hands. The group then proceeds to the question and answer segment of their presentation and Jasmine says that she will start with a question or statement and wants to get the class' response:

Jasmine: Do you think that justice is denied to North Bay High students? Do you agree that it's not fair that we're treated like prisoners here just from 8:20 to 3:10 because they receive money for every foot that steps in the door instead of treating us like striving individuals who want to better ourselves in education? When students walk into classes, teachers don't see faces, just dollar signs around our necks. What do you feel about that?

Jasmine has, from a sound textual analysis of this question, extrapolated the findings to then analyze, question, and critique her own world. The directions to the groups were to ask questions to facilitate discussion around the texts (film and novel). Initially I was shocked by the question and doubted its appropriateness but soon realized, from the responses, that this was a textual question. I had worked so diligently to help the students see their world as a powerful source of knowledge for confronting texts that, to them, their world had indeed become text. In Jasmine's eyes, as she would later admit, this was the only logical question to ask at this point in the unit and in the class. The students had been identifying particularly with Carl Lee and the African American community throughout the film; so it was natural that they would, in analyzing whether this man received justice, also analyze their own lives to determine whether their treatment as students and citizens was just. Jasmine's initial question elicits a wave of responses from her peers:

Robin: I agree, I totally agree. I really don't feel that it's right because we don't receive any justice. We come here to learn and we think we're coming into . . . like a home. When you come home . . . you expect your mom to . . . like greet you or whatever. You expect the best. And when you come to school, you expect the best education that you can get. But while you have administrators and what not telling you to stay in one spot and not helping you, no . . . no . . . we don't receive justice at all.

Viet: I think it's pretty much all face and appearance for the school to have all these kids inside school. You know . . . when they lock the doors, chain the doors, it's just for, . . . like . . . face to compete with these other schools so they can look the same as these other schools.

These other students, as a result of Jasmine's question, are also able to make ample critiques of the school system and its failure to give fair and equal treatment to the students. Each gives an opinion and then justifies their opinion with an example and explanation of that example, just as if they were carrying out a traditional textual argument. Robin makes use of a metaphor when she compares the school with a home and contextualizes her argument by referring to what she feels to be apathetic administrators.

Jasmine's second question, which consumes the duration of the period, is "What does justice look like in our society?"

Robin: Justice is freedom and I . . . I . . . don't feel I have freedom. They say I can say anything I want but I know if I was to walk in the president's office and say, "this is unfair" (sucks her teeth and makes a hand gesture like the police traffic signal for stopping) you need to be quiet. We have a right to learn . . . if you go into a teacher's face and say that, we don't have that right!

Chan: Police are just like teachers. They drive all around like teachers walk all round. They don't care. They just don't care!

At this point Chan suggests that the class move beyond merely talking about these issues and the group spends the remainder of the period discussing their plans for the final 6 weeks to help bring justice to the students of North Bay High.

It is worth noting that, after this final presentation, the class chose to devote the final 6 weeks to creating a magazine that would expose the injustices of North Bay High School. *Serious Voices From Knowledgeable Youth* raised quite a stir around campus as various administrators, campus supervisors, and teachers were approached and interviewed. A companion video essay was completed and it, along with a petition of grievances, was sent to local television stations. The students were able to see their story aired on the local news and, with the notoriety, were also able to secure an audience with all of the major candidates for mayor that year.

Throughout the units during the discussions, presentations, and debates, the class, in retrospect, seemed naturally headed for this sort of response. Several key incidents, indeed, foreshadowed it. Establishing powerful, critical connections between the popular world and the academic curriculum ensures that the knowledge created will not remain confined within the classroom walls. It will necessarily spill out into the real world to deal with real issues.

I feel it important to begin this final section with some disclaimers. First of all, I have not presented this unit as a cookie-cutter solution to all of the ills in urban education. Clearly, my students, as many others in similar situations, faced myriad problems and obstacles that hindered them from achieving their potential. Also, the class was by no means perfect. Students were occasionally disengaged and, for some, truancy remained a large problem. Furthermore, I understand that not everyone who attempts this unit will achieve the same results. I recognize that the relationships forged between teachers and students are at least as important as the choice of curriculum.

What I have attempted to demonstrate is that students already possess many of the skills that we, as educators want to impart to them. However, by not allowing them to tap into their huge reservoirs of knowledge, we also prevent many from incorporating these skills into their engagements with traditional texts. The insertion of contemporary film along with a dialogic, problem-posing format of discussion and student-led presentations allows students to tap into that reservoir and provides a powerful pathway into such canonical texts as *The Odyssey* and *Native Son*. Not only were students able to make profound connections between their world and the text, but also they imbibed these texts with life and established relevance between the texts and their world. Penelope and Bigger Thomas became icons for contemporary discussions of gender and race. This, for me, was an unexpected benefit and represented a fundamental shift from reading a text to interrogating one.

There are several profound implications of this study for educators and researchers alike. What I encourage are creative approaches to instruction that emanate from the worlds and perceptions of the students and are based upon a sound theoretical framework. This will not occur without a serious reconsideration of what constitutes effective instruction. Such reconsideration must be predicated on the belief that all students possess knowledge and talents that traditional education may or may not reveal. I also hope that readers recognize the tremendous potential of incorporating popular film into the curriculum for increasing motivation, tapping into background knowledge, improving awareness, and, yes, fostering a sociopolitical philosophy. It can also provide students with a model for how to understand and critique their own world.

Creating the opportunities and forums for teacher-initiated critical research in which educators can conduct research projects such as this one and share their findings with other teachers, challenging them to critically reflect upon their own pedagogy may prove a fundamental step in revolutionizing classroom instruction and transforming urban schools into places where both students and teachers feel empowered as intellectuals and change agents (Freire, 1998; Giroux, 1988). Critical theorists believe that research is an ethical and political act (Apple, 1979; Bodkin and Biklen, 1998; Carspecken, 1996; Kincheloe and McLaren, 1998). Critical research is intended to engage and benefit those who are marginalized in society. Along these lines, educators can employ critical research to empower individuals traditionally marginalized within the educational discourse while also confronting the injustice of a particular society or sphere within the society (McLaren, 1994). Critical research thus used by urban teachers becomes a transformational endeavor unembarrassed by the label "political" and unafraid to consummate a relationship with an emancipatory consciousness (Carspecken, 1996; Kincheloe and McLaren, 1998).

Critical researchers often regard their work as a first step toward forms of political action that can redress the injustices found in the field site or constructed in the very act of research itself. Thus, as critical researchers, educators can enter into investigations with their assumptions and positionality as interested insiders on the table, so no one is confused concerning the epistemological and political baggage they bring with them to the research site. Critical research considers education to be a social institution designed for social and cultural reproduction and transformation (Merriam, 1998). Therefore, drawing from Marxist philosophy, critical theory, and feminist theory, knowledge generated by educators through this mode of research becomes an ideological critique of power, privilege, and oppression in areas of educational practice. As critical ethnographers of education, literacy educators can use critical qualitative research to collect data about schooling practices and their relation to the social order to ultimately undermine or transform that order while avoiding the pitfalls of sociological objectivity and functionalism and giving room to the critical voices of urban youth that are often absent from traditional research (Bodkan and Biklen 1998; Carspecken, 1996; Denzin and Lincoln, 1998). I will talk at greater length about the processes and purposes of critical research in the final chapter.

Considerations When Teaching Popular Film

I have also explored the potential of film and television with pre-service and practicing teachers in my role as a teacher educator at Michigan State University. In my most recent English methods course, for example, we focused on the use of popular culture and critical literary theories in diverse classrooms. The pre-service teachers were excited about the possibilities of creating lessons that interested and related to students while simultaneously satisfying district and state curriculum standards. For their class assignments and lab teaching episodes, these pre-service teachers used Marxists, feminists, and postcolonial lenses to analyze films such as *Apocalypse Now* and *Remember the Titans*.

Through the years, however, I have learned that the excitement over the use of film and television does not always translate into transformed classroom practice. In my experiences at conferences and workshops, I have encountered veteran teachers who are aware of the possibilities, yet feel that they will not be able to sway colleagues and parents. One of my primary aims in presentations, workshops, and classes is to help teachers feel comfortable about communicating the rationale for their practice to multiple constituencies, including other teachers, administrators, parents, and students.

When explaining non-traditional classroom practices, it is important to help relevant audiences understand how innovative classroom instruction can also increase students' academic literacies. Every chance that I get, I encourage teachers to explain how their classroom activities fulfill standards as stated in district, state, and national frameworks. It is quite simple, for instance, to discuss the critical study of film and television within the National Council of Teachers of English/International Reading Association (NCTE/IRA) Standards for English Language Arts (1996). It is also important for teachers to understand that they do not operate in a vacuum, but in a context that is often hostile to film. Debunking preconceived notions of film and television and erasing historical images of their use in English classrooms are not overnight projects. There may even be colleagues on the faculty who still use film and television in reductive ways.

Teaching popular television and film in secondary English classrooms is a vital and valuable enterprise for many reasons. Not only can this practice help to improve academic reading and writing, it can also facilitate more critical student engagement with popular media. This is especially important, given the tremendous influence that these media have on the identity development of youth. Armed with feminist, Marxist, and postcolonial lenses, secondary students can become more empowered over their readings of film and television texts and maybe even more selective consumers of these texts as well. I am also holding on to the possibility of a few budding filmmakers emerging from these classrooms with products that deserve much celebration for accurately depicting the social world in all its complexities.

Chapter 6

Teaching Mass Media

Vignettes From Practice

Vignette #1

Four high school teens who are studying the relationship between urban youth and the mass media have been granted an interview with several reporters and editors from a major daily newspaper. During the interview the teens ask pointed questions about the lack of positive coverage for teens of color. John, one of the students, asks whether a violent incident during the Democratic National Convention involving young people would be more newsworthy than a story covering youth engaged in socially just activity. "Of course," one reporter responds, "if it bleeds, it leads."

Vignette #2

It is August 14, 2000, the first day of the Democratic National Convention. The seminar students and I are seated in the upstairs choir room at a church in downtown Los Angeles near the headquarters of the convention. In preparation for our day's activities, we are examining "dailies" (major daily newspapers) from across the country. The

---

cont.

students have honed in on the cover of the Los Angeles Times, which features a protest that many of the students attended. The picture features a blonde girl of maybe four or five surrounded by four police officers wearing riot gear. The students are angered at the obvious parallels to the famous picture of a little black girl attempting to enter a previously segregated school taken during the civil rights movement. They are also angry that the juxtaposition of images is being used to justify police force against them, teen activists interested in social change. A lively and critical discussion ensues before we take to the streets to conduct our research.

Vignette #3

LaShonda and Melissa, two student representatives of the Access to Media group have actually obtained access to members of the national media that are covering the convention. With surveys, tape recorders, and notebooks in hand, they approach these professionals in hopes of gathering data for their research project. Though taken aback, most of the media representatives oblige the young researchers. Several minutes into the activity, police arrive on the scene to escort the young women and their colleagues away from the media center. They attempt in vain to explain that they have legitimate access to the location. As they are being led away the team attempts to interview the police officers, who refuse the invitation.

Mass Media in the Lives of Urban Youth

Most people spend as much as one-third of their lives engaged with mass media. A person of 60 years of age has seen, read, or heard as many as 50 million advertisements (Sardar and Van Loon, 2000). The sheer volume of time and involvement makes the mass media at least as viable a pedagogical institution as schools and speaks to the importance of these media to America's youth (Giroux, 1996). Whole departments have opened up at universities around the globe dedicated solely to the study of media and their impact on the human condition. Indeed, media and cultural studies are emerging as the postmodern discipline. Some pundits and philosophers predict that the English departments of the twenty-first century will look more and more like media and cultural studies departments. Whether these predictions actually come to fruition, few can deny the importance or relevance of this new topic of inquiry. Kellner and Durham, in their introduction to *Media and Cultural Studies* (2000) report:

> Forms of media culture provide role and gender models, fashion hints, life-style images, and icons of personality. The narratives of media culture offer patterns of proper and improper behavior, moral messages, and ideological conditioning, sugar-coating social and political ideas with pleasurable and seductive forms of popular entertainment. . . . With media and culture playing such important roles in contemporary life, it is obvious that we must come to understand our cultural environment if we want control over our lives. (p. 1)

This chapter focuses mostly on the critical consumption of media advertising and major news reporting, two of the most pervasive and influential forms of the mass media most commonly associated with the term "media," which itself is not an unproblematic term. Though film, television, and music are also popular media, I have chosen to deal with these in separate chapters that focus more specifically on narrative and genre than representations of mass media.

A recent report by the National Reading Conference on literacy development among adolescents (Alvermann, 2001) calls for literacy educators to help students learn to more critically interrogate the mass media that play such a central role in their identity development and worldview. In this way, teaching the mass media is also an approach that can simultaneously promote academic and critical literacies. In order to function as empowered citizens with positive self concepts, teens need to be able to deconstruct and reinterpret the messages that are sent to them by media advertisers. At the same time, with the proliferation of independent news sources coupled with the concentration of news reporting agencies, these same youth need the analytical skills—the literacy skills—that enable them to make sense of the mixed and multiple messages about the world that are conveyed through the various news media. Young people need to understand the difference between reality and the media's various representations of reality and that media representations themselves reflect ideologies and stances about the world. The news is not neutral and it is not innocuous. Individuals wishing to remain informed need to learn to "read" news media carefully; they must also triangulate traditional readings with counter-readings of media texts. Critical citizens must also be producers of media texts writing or using other images when and where they can, whether through a web page, a community newsletter, a brochure, an independent newspaper, a letter to the editor, or a message sent out on a listserv.

The British Broadcasting Standards commission has recommended that media studies be taught at primary school, given its importance to students' lives (Sardar and Van Loon, 2000). I contend in this chapter that secondary schools in the United States are also ideal sites for media and cultural studies. I examined data gathered during a summer program I coordinated in which urban teens were apprenticed as critical researchers studying urban youth's access to public spaces and social institutions. One research team decided to study urban youth's access to the corporate media and the corporate media's portrayal of urban youth. To attack their research question, these students read relevant literature relating to critical media literacy and the sociology of education, designed a study, conducted interviews, analyzed countless hours of news coverage, and performed a content analysis of major daily newspapers from across the nation. This chapter follows these teens through their research process looking at the implications of this process for their literacy development and literacy education.

Youth Access to Media:
A Critical Intervention

Entitled, "Education, Access, and Democracy in Los Angeles: LA Youth and Convention 2000," this summer research seminar was designed to apprentice urban youth as critical researchers of urban issues in the context of the Democratic National Convention. Other goals of the research seminar were to develop and demonstrate research and literacy skills needed for success in college and to promote critical awareness and a commitment to research and social justice.

To these ends, the seminar involved 30 urban youth from the Greater Los Angeles area, graduate students, and university faculty in a 4-week program. The first 2 weeks focused on research apprenticeship. At the university's law school, the students worked with their team leaders and faculty researchers as they learned about the basics of critical research and were introduced to relevant literature from social theory. During the 3rd week, which corresponded to the Democratic National Convention (DNC), students assembled downtown in a Pico Union church to be close to the DNC and its surrounding activities. Students encountered and interviewed prominent politicians, community leaders, corporate representatives, media personnel, and activists. They also participated in the Shadow Convention, a progressive alternative to the traditional convention, and attended a live broadcast of "Democracy Live," a show featuring young people involved in the political process. Finally, the students were given the opportunity to observe and participate in a series of protests and marches in downtown Los Angeles, most notably the "Human Need not Corporate Greed. March for Our Lives."

Returning to the university for the final week of the seminar, students and team leaders worked to assemble and analyze the data collected during the convention in preparation for final reports and presentations, which would take place at the end of the week. On the final day of the seminar, these students presented their work to an audience of parents, teachers, community leaders, university faculty members, and media representatives.

One group, in particular, decided to examine youth access to media and media access to youth. They began with the premise that millions of people rely on the mainstream media every day, perhaps without critical analysis. They were also concerned that youth were not portrayed positively or representative of majority of the population in mainstream media. After a few initial meetings during which these students addressed their own experiences and concerns and read central texts, they devised the following research questions:

- What is the media's presentation of youth issues and/or youth protesters?
- How does the media's framing of youth, youth issues, and/or youth protesters compare to youth reality?

Led by their instructor, the research group conducted a review of relevant literature as they prepared to design their study. They read such complex works as Douglas Kellner's (1995) *Media Culture: Cultural Studies; Identity and Politics Between the Modern and the*

Postmodern Media Culture and Peter McLaren's *Rethinking Media Literacy: A Critical Pedagogy of Representation*. From their review of the literature, the research group developed working definitions of complex terms related to the critical investigation of media culture. For example, *critical media literacy* was defined as the ability to obtain facts from the media text necessary to examine, ask questions, analyze, and critically dissect all the forms of culture, language, issues of power, and positionality within a text that may create particular meanings, and identities, and to shape and transform the material and social conditions of our culture and society. Other components of critical media literacy include

- Questioning reality vs. media-induced perception;
- Examining who should be considered the experts on a particular topic;
- Problematizing the most accurate, reliable, and factual source of information from the different types of resources or media; and
- Exploring how their culture, society, and polity are structured and work through media representations.

The media group defined *corporate media* as large, city-based mainstream papers/media companies that are organized on the model of mass production and is produced for a mass audience according to genres/language used. Another important term, the *entertainment media*, was defined as media that is solely used to entertain and which is not always factual. Entertainment media are often highly pleasurable and use sight, sound, and spectacle to seduce audiences into identifying with certain views, attitudes, feelings, and positions. Consumer culture offers a dazzling array of goods and services that induce individuals to pursue commercial gratification at all costs. The group also felt it important to focus on media language, which they saw as published words that evoke history, culture, power, positionality, race, class, gender, and so on and are rarely ever neutral.

The group also created important diagrams and organizers to present and make sense of their emerging theoretical perspective, both to themselves and to prospective audiences. The *Insider-Outsider Circle* was a diagram showing how the person on the inside often has the power, voice, and more access to influence the lives of the outsiders and how outsiders live and see a situation. The *Media Optic* referred to the way the media views events, incidents, facts, who are the experts, what voices and stories are heard, the complexity of a situation or themes, and what effects how media views the phenomenon. Finally, the *Media Filter* explains how the media interprets, filters, and frames a phenomenon with some examination of how the media's positionality, corporate structures, marketing strategies, finance backers, and other components may influence what stories are told, what voices are heard, and who benefits from the story.

At this point, the group was ready to begin their study. They created surveys for the general public and the media (see Appendix G). The data collection took place at the university, the Shadow Convention, Staples Center, *Democracy Live* taping, Pershing Square, the Marriott Hotel, and in students' communities. The survey data were then coded and analyzed through a computer software program. The students also conducted numerous individual and focus group interviews with media representatives and public officials.

The media group also performed an extensive content analysis of major daily newspapers that were published during the week of the convention. In particular, they examined five mainstream media papers (USA Today, New York Times, Washington Post, LA Times, Chicago Tribune. and a community paper La Opinion) all printed on Tuesday, August 15th (which reported the opening day of the convention) to examine how the media framed youth activists, demonstrators, and concertgoers who were asked to leave a concert/protest area by police (see Table 6-1).

The surveys revealed that, although local community papers, friends, family members, national newspapers, TV news, and radio programming were heavily relied upon resources by individuals, the most accurate and factual resource was considered by many to be their own lived experience. Further, this group found that 40% of the media personnel and general public believed most recent stories or themes around youth depict that of violence, drugs, alcohol, and teens out of control. The focus group interviews revealed that there are passive and active roles that media takes and some stories are pre-selected before events actually occur. The group also learned that there are differences in resources and investigation given to different topics depending on perceived importance and marketability to target audiences.

Finally, through their interviews with media personnel, their examination of daily newspaper and their personal experiences, this group was able to document the existence of pre-packaged , "if it

Table 6-1. Sample Newspaper Analysis (Media Group)			
Newspaper on August 15	Word Count	Coverage of Youth Activist/ Protest Issues	Pictures
USA Today	Weapons – 13 Police – 6 Fire – 1 Protester –5 Students –0 Youth - 1	None	At nighttime, four protesters surround a fire, two with handkerchiefs covering their mouths. One protester is putting a piece of paper in the fire out of the 8000 youth at concert/demonstration area.
LA Times	Weapons – 2 Police – 20 Arrest – 2 Riot – 5 Protester – 4 Youth – 2 Gas Masks – 1 Students – 2	None	Five cops of color walking in the middle of the street with riot gear preparing for any riots that may break out.
Chicago Tribune	Protester – 22 Violence – 7 Weapons – 5 Police – 27 Fire –1 Anarchists - 2	Two issues mentioned: "Human need not corporate greed" and Occidental Petroleum Inc.	Six LADP officers in riot gear with batons are on top of a protester who is trying to cover his head with his arms.
LA Opinion	Protester – 2 Police – 7 Manifestantes – 12 Disturbance – 1	Three issues mentioned: Oil drilling, nuclear weapons, and spending money on schools.	Three pictures: one cop hitting one person, calm protesters walking and holding signs, and a picture of other calm demonstrators.

bleeds, it leads" stories. For example, the members of the research team actually participated in a peaceful and powerful march through the streets of downtown Los Angeles only to see the same minor flare up reported as the leading story in five different major papers across the country. The story was actually inaccurately reported in a similar fashion in all of the papers with the same photos and almost identical captions. A local reporter commented off the record that editors at his paper were waiting for the story and already had the headlines ready to go before the event took place. The tenor of his comment was that there was bound to be at least one incident of resistance or violence that the papers could ship out to the rest of the country to fit with their narrative of the convention. Nowhere in any of the papers was the purpose of the march mentioned or any of the issues that the activists were marching for. As a matter of fact, the research group was never able to identify activists with particular causes through any of the major daily newspapers that week. Activists, called protestors, were linked to violence and disobedience, but were not identified as citizens who cared deeply about freedom, justice, and democracy.

The group concluded that many students have a tendency to read and interact with mainstream media without questioning the perspective, the experience, the truth, the author's positionality, and the expertise of others, let alone how it might affect students in the process of identity formation to determine how they saw themselves and how they interact with others. Further, the research group felt that most teens failed to consider how decisions are made in the media regarding youth, youth issues, and youth activists. It is highly possible, they argued, that in the process of accessing various types of media (i.e., newspapers, television shows, internet, and radio, in addition to what they learn from peers, family members, communities, and from other forms of text), many students may consciously or unconsciously question and/or learn what it means, for example, to be stereotyped and silenced in the United States from those whose language evokes a particular history, position of power, and oppression over others.

Given media coverage and the structure of many stories will likely remain unchanged, they contended that students be instilled with a more critical awareness of the language, social construction of identity, and knowledge of how race/ethnicity relations is discussed in media. In particular, they encouraged students to critically think, raise questions as to what factors may affect who students think they are, what they can become, how they think of others, how students interact with others, to examine issues of power, and to analyze relationships, particularly African American and Latino youth relations. Students, they argued, need to be trained in critical media literacy and seen as experts on youth to be empowered to change the future for the better.

These research findings corroborated the experiences of the researchers both before and during the Democratic National Convention. Both media and police profiled youth to be violent protestors including the students themselves as they circulated through the convention headquarters attempting to gather data. Most importantly, though, the research findings represent the absolutely phenomenal work young people are capable of when given the opportunity and tools to investigate issues, such as media culture, that are immediately relevant to their everyday lives. It can certainly be argued that, during this process, students learned and used many skills that would serve them well as active citizens and as participants in the new economy and in civil society.

Considerations When Teaching Mass Media

The media provide an ideal context for teachers to talk about writing for empowerment. Teachers and students can work together to create a class web site or newsletter that provides counter-narratives of reality. Teachers also can have students write letters to the editor about topics and stories that are important to their lives. Students that are visually or artistically inclined can create socially minded advertising campaigns that promote wellness, environmental conservation, or positive self-images.

Students can also perform market research on commercials or comparative analyses of news broadcasts, daily newspapers, or advertisements looking for biases, or redundant themes, or harmful portrayals of individuals or groups. Bronwyn Williams (2002) discusses writing activities associated with "critical" television viewing. His college writing activities involved students watching commercials as a class to determine what group was being advertised to and critiquing overt and covert messages sent by advertisers. Building on the work of Williams, teachers can have students critically examine mass media advertising noting portrayals of certain gender, ethnic, socioeconomic, and sexually oriented groups. Finally, students can interview members of the news media as did our students in their project during the summer research seminar.

It is clear that mainstream media plays a pervasive role in the young people's construction of self and construction of society. It is unconscionable that so little attention is paid to the organization, function, and impact of the media in traditional secondary classrooms. As educators, we really need to ask ourselves what curricula could possibly be more important than critical media studies. The onus must really shift to educators to prove that classical and traditional curricula are more important to the everyday lives and future welfare of their students that justifies their current practices. I encourage postmodern teacher-activists to question and challenge these traditional practices in favor of curricula that are more able to connect with students' lives and motivate them to undertake the kind of work that was demonstrated in this chapter.

I would go further in encouraging literacy educators to not only enable students to become critical consumers of media texts, but to provide the opportunities for students to become critical producers of counter-media texts. Whenever possible, schools should be creating newsletters, pamphlets, brochures, web sites, radio stations, and television broadcasts that portray young people in the roles of cultural producers. What could be more fruitful for motivating students to read and write than knowing their stories will be shared with larger audiences and could play a part in initiating social change?

Chapter 7

Teaching Popular Sports

Vignettes From Practice

Vignette #1

I am working with the South Bay High Project students in their morning tutoring class. Claude, one of the students, produces a copy of a best-selling biography of a famous professional wrestler. Several other boys express an interest in reading the text and the book is not without an interested reader for the remainder of the period. Two hours later, I am observing in Claude's English 11 class, which has a silent reading period. Claude again brandishes his book and reads intently for the duration of the reading period. For two hours, Claude, who had been described as uninterested in reading, is clearly fascinated and engaged with a 500+ page book written which is at a fairly sophisticated level.

Vignette #2

Fourteen participants on the women's varsity basketball team enter the team room with their binders ready for inspection. These 14–17 year-olds have been asked to assemble binders that include: diagrams of offensive and defensive sets, individual and team goals, academic schedules, and copies of famous coaching philosophies such as Pat Summit's Dirty Dozen and John Wooden's Pyramid of Success. The

---

cont.

girls are also asked to memorize the Dirty Dozen and have been quiz-zing each other in preparation for the tests given frequently during and after practice. Many of these student-athletes also possess scores of sports magazines and local newspapers that have predicted them to finish among the top 25 teams in the area.

Vignette #3

Caleb is a defensive lineman and struggling student described by some teachers and counselors as non-literate. I have been assigned to tutor Caleb to help him develop academic skills. To one tutoring session, Caleb brings the sports page from a local newspaper. I ask what he's up to and he shows me the lines for the Saturday college football games and proceeds to explain his own picks for the weekend. For the sake of argument, I entertain him in argument about his predictions and he shows me that he has basically annotated the paper and augmented its analysis with his own substantial experience watching these teams in action. I explain to him the similarities between his hobby and the literacy and critical argument skills he needs to complete his writing assignments for his classes.

Popular Sports in the Lives of Urban Youth

It may seem surprising that I would advocate teaching popular sports to literacy educators. Unfortunately, sports have been cast as the antithesis of academics, as activity that has little to do with literacy development. I say unfortunately because so many teens are involved with sports, whether as athletes or fans. Thirty years of Title IX legislation have opened up sports participation to girls and young women, whose numbers are increasing all of the time. Now there are even magazines, such as *Sports Illustrated for Women*, that cater to this growing market. Cable television with stations such as ESPN and Fox Sports World deliver sports action and commentary to awaiting fans 24 hours a day, 7 days a week. The proliferation of sports magazines and the internet web sites targeted toward young fans have ensured that sports are prominent in the world of teens.

Although they are much maligned in schools, or associated with selfish or delinquent athletes in the popular media, there are many positive impacts of sports participation for secondary and postsecondary athletes. Athletes, for instance, have been shown to have higher graduation rates and better grades than their non-participatory peers. Research reports on young girls' participation in sports have found that involvement in organized sports increases positive body image and self-esteem while decreasing the incidence of teen pregnancy and substance abuse. These outcomes are not to be taken lightly during an era where many of our young women are plagued by these social ills.

We have known for some time that sports involvement teaches young women and men the skills of teamwork, cooperation, delayed gratification, and sacrificing self-interest for the greater good of the team. The relationships developed among athletes and between athletes and coaches are some of the strongest bonds kids form while at school. Major corporations are inclined to hire former athletes because they have cultivated many of the skills needed to work cooperatively in today's global village. In fact, athletes, more than many others, have found ways to work together across multiple lines of difference including race, ethnicity, religion, and socioeconomic status.

Sports participation is so crucial to students' mental, physical, and emotional well being as well as the betterment of society, that many teachers, parents, and coaches have recommended that participation be viewed as a curricular activity rather than an extracurricular one. It is also the argument of this chapter that the literacy practices associated with interest or involvement in sports can be drawn upon to develop academic skills.

Critical Interventions Involving the use of Popular Sports

I chose examples from my career as a coach as well as a tutor at an Athletic Study Center because, unfortunately, I didn't use sports as much as I should have to promote literacy development in my own English classes, given the preferences and expertise of my students. In the fall of 1996, a fellow English teacher and I found ourselves as the head coaches of a struggling girl's basketball program at North Bay High. I say "found" because neither of us had any intention of coaching until we were asked by our students to take it on. That semester, we also enrolled as graduate students in the Language, Literacy, and Culture program at a nearby university where we learned about the importance of affirming and drawing upon the language and literacy practices associated with everyday activity to promote school-based literacies. We decided that if we were going to coach, we would not only create a winning team, but we would take advantage of the girls' interest in basketball to develop them as successful students. With these multiple goals in mind, we created several facets of the program specifically to facilitate the learning of academic and critical literacies.

I also took an evening job at the Athletic Study Center at this same university. Through a joint program with the School of Education, a program was created that targeted the most "at-risk" athletes in the program to teach them the study and survival skills they needed to succeed in school. Given my background as a college athlete and my interests in literacy and popular culture, I thought this would be a valuable experience. Besides, the additional stipend didn't hurt either! But, I was right. I learned a great deal from my time with these young athletes that influenced my perspective on the relationship between sports participation and literacy development. I should say, though, that all of the athletes I worked with in the study center were males not because there were no female athletes in academic jeopardy. The creators of the program really strove to have male tutors work with male athletes and female tutors with female athletes, as some of the issues inhibiting academic performance were gender specific.

Reading Sport

Originally in our classroom and later a team room, we created an athletic and literacy-filled sanctuary for the girls. We inundated these sanctuaries with print. We bought magazines, newspapers, season guides, and how-to books and tapes. We purchased books written by famous coaches and former athletes that became required reading. We also acquired as much text as we could on the then-fledgling WNBA including media guides and stories about individual players and teams. We also wrote to college coaches across the country (more than 300 letters) asking them to send schedules, media guides, and information regarding admissions requirements and major offerings. Most wrote back enabling us to amass an impressive library of basketball and college-preparatory materials.

We also used our leverage as coaches to encourage our athletes to read in their academic subjects as well. We promoted a team goal of maintaining a 3.5 grade point average in college-preparatory classes. We met this goal on several occasions. To facilitate this goal, we held a mandatory academic study hall that met three times a week for two hours. As English teachers, we used our expertise to assist the students with their literacy needs while recruiting volunteers from our faculty colleagues and university undergraduates to work with students in other subjects.

At the Athletic Study Center, I was working with Caleb, a college football player who regarded himself as semi-literate. I believe his actual words were, "I can't read!" I knew that Caleb could read, and I was fairly certain that he knew that he could read, too. I took Caleb's comment to mean that he could not read and relate to texts in a manner that would earn him academic credit. He had every right to believe this given his sordid academic history.

On almost every occasion that I saw him, though, Caleb had a copy of the sports page. This was no pristine well-folded sports page either. It was crumpled, dog-eared, torn, and even annotated at times. Caleb used the paper to keep track of his former high school, which wasn't too far away, and to keep track of the latest developments in college and professional football. As time wore on and I developed a relationship with Caleb, I got in the habit of asking him about his old school and the football world. He would use the paper as a map and act as my tour guide through the world of sports. I learned that Caleb possessed almost encyclopedic knowledge of the more than 100 NCAA Division I football teams, meaning that he could identify them by conference, run down their starting lineups, their coaches, their records, and their upcoming opponents. He could also add some critical commentary about the team, the direction they were headed, and why his beloved team could "take them apart."

Caleb was reading and relating to texts in a way that should have garnered him academic recognition. I wish I could say that I made these connections explicitly with Caleb all the time, but I didn't. I encouraged him to read the newspaper and talk about sports because it made him feel good and smart to share his expert knowledge with the teacher turned student. I occasionally made connections between sports knowledge and writing, as I will relate later in this chapter, but it wasn't nearly as systematic or exhaustive as it could have been.

Years later, I would encounter the work of Jeffrey Wilhelm (1997) who reminds English teachers that our kids' texts may not be our texts. We may find their selections immature, odious, redundant, poorly written, or even mildly offensive, but the point is to let students begin with texts that they enjoy, find relevant, and can easily manage. Our job, he argues, is to encourage and affirm students as readers. There will be times when we introduce them to our texts, but we must also allow them time and space to revel in theirs. If I, or any of Caleb's other English teachers had done this, he might not have thought so poorly of himself as a reader.

Writing Sport

There were several facets to the writing associated with participation in the basketball program, such as: taking notes on great players scouting potential opponents, maintaining a playbook, and writing goal sheets. My colleague and I would make a habit of videotaping every televised basketball game we could, especially those that involved women. Of particular interest were the University of Tennessee Lady Volunteers coached by Pat Summit. This team was in the process of putting together a 39-0 season and winning their third straight NCAA Women's Basketball championship. Periodically, we would meet as a team to watch a big game that we had videotaped. While watching as a team, we would stop the tape occasionally to have conversations about particular players and situations. We wanted the girls to begin thinking like basketball intellectuals and we also wanted outstanding play and championship character modeled for the young women. It was expected that all of the players would have their issued binders and would jot down notes during these team viewings.

We also had the policy that any of the players could check out a single videotape of a game at a time for as long as a week. Our athletes would check out these tapes to focus on a particular athlete who played their position or maybe just to watch an outstanding player such as Chamique Holdsclaw. During these private, at-home viewings, the girls would take notes, evaluating the strengths and weaknesses of these players while simultaneously commenting on how they could augment their own nascent games. If I knew that an athlete had checked out a certain tape, I would ask to see the notes and engage them in conversation about their viewing. I might even encourage them to watch the tape a second time and take better notes.

Another important component of any winning basketball program is the ability to scout and successfully prepare for upcoming opponents. If we were participating in a tournament, we might have the opportunity to watch our opponents in action. Otherwise, we would have a parent or other volunteer tape the game. In some way, shape, or form, we would either watch or get tape on serious opponents.

During the scouting sessions, our girls would normally focus on athletes who played a similar position—the girl they would have to guard, who was also the player who would be trying to stop them as well. Our veteran players would create a checklist of questions to ask of each player: Is she right or left-handed? What is her favorite move? Does she rebound well? How does she play defense? What other strengths and weaknesses does she possess? Some of our girls would also chart shots on particular players or keep other statistical information while scouting. Collaborative meetings with our players during which these notes were compared and shared would form an important core of our scouting report.

In order to fully prepare, however, we needed to prepare for more than just individual athletes, we needed to know how they functioned as an entire team. This involved diagramming offenses, defenses, and presses. Two or three days before a big game, our girls would have to learn a whole new system and our strategy to disrupt this system. This required the girls to memorize pages of notes and diagrams within a relatively short period. Over the course of their careers, our girls would have dozens of pages of copious notes on our most bitter and respected rivals.

The most important and comprehensive task that the young women faced was mastering our own complicated system, which included multiple offenses, defenses, presses, press breaks, and out of bounds plays. Every girl would keep her own playbook, in which each set would be diagrammed and annotated, most notably with her own individual responsibilities highlighted. Each diagram would also have to represent a host of contingencies. There are many if–then statements associated with basketball play. To quote a famous coaching slogan, "you take what they'll give you." As the season progressed, we would need to make changes, additions, and adjustments to the system, requiring the girls to maintain a running commentary.

A separate section of the playbook was reserved for team rules, goals, and ethics. Athletes were expected to write statements of athletic, personal, and academic goals. There were also various coaching and living philosophies that the girls were expected to write down and commit to memory. We conducted periodic checks to see that all facets of the playbook were kept current.

With the young men from the Athletic Study Center, I realized that I could draw upon their extensive experience with sport to help them with college-level writing. For instance, one of the most important skills students need is the ability to use various rhetorical strategies to make persuasive arguments. Many of the athletes were getting feedback from their instructors suggesting that they were having difficulties developing arguments. I knew that these young men knew how to make and defend arguments, they just were not aware of the rhetorical moves they made in their everyday lives as young people and as athletes. For example, it is a favorite pastime of athletes, fans, and commentators to predict and debate the probable outcomes of sporting events. Within these debates, participants use all of the three appeals identified by Aristotle in classical rhetoric: appeals to reason (logos), to emotion (pathos), and to the speaker's authority (ethos).

My chagrin at the negative feedback and my belief in these young men provided enough of an impetus to hatch an idea. During our next tutoring session, I challenged these young men to their very core. I knew enough about college football to make the case that their upcoming opponents were a superior team and would beat them soundly. I simply told the athletes that I thought their opponents were going to win. Needless to say, a fierce and impassioned, yet sophisticated argument ensued that employed classical and modern rhetorical strategies. To each point that the athletes offered, I offered a counterpoint that seemed equally logical. The athletes responded with charts, diagrams, special plays, coverages, secondary sources such as newspapers, statistics, emotional appeals to school pride, and appeals to their status as insiders and football experts to prove me wrong, shut me up, or run me off campus!

Once the argument had run its course, I handed back their compositions and jokingly intimated that they didn't know how to argue. They got it. They also became excited about what we had done, which enabled me to explain the complex moves they made rhetorically to win the argument. I then gave them each the assignment to write a composition making the argument that they would defeat University X in the upcoming football game. After they had completed and revised their compositions, I had them give copies to their instructors. I could see a noticeable change in the comments on successive pieces and all of the athletes that participated passed their college writing course.

Deconstructing Through Sport

There is another important reading activity associated with interest or participation in sports. It is not the same type of reading as decoding words on the page, though it is no less significant in the lives of students. Throughout my career as an educator, I have attempted to use young people's affinity with sports to engender critical readings of the world—informed ways of reading the world as if it were a text. Indeed, critical literacy theorists like Paulo Freire (1997) contend that an authentic reading of the world precede a reading of the word. At the very least, I see these as coordinated and interrelated activities.

For the girls on my basketball team, participation in competitive sports provided an ideal site to struggle against limiting gender roles for women that proliferate through mass media and are even supported by public institutions such as schools (Orenstein, 1995). Through participation in basketball, the girls learned that it was possible and advantageous for women to be competitive and assertive. Indeed, in order to succeed on the basketball court in a large gymnasium filled with noisy fans, one must literally yell and demand to be heard. I saw several of my athletes find their voices in that gymnasium along with other habits of mind and heart that would serve them well in classrooms, in boardrooms, and other spaces where the odds would be stacked against them.

The girls also learned to love their broad shoulders and muscular arms. They learned to covet and embrace adjectives such as strong and tough. I am certain that I witnessed changes in the postures of several of my taller athletes who proudly flaunted their size, which was a definite advantage on the basketball court, signifying a new reading of themselves and their surrounding environment. Perhaps this is not a reading that can be directly measured on a standardized test, but it is also not one that is insignificant to our goals as literacy educators.

Most importantly, these girls learned to share their basketball feminism with the younger girls and boys throughout the city that loved the game and adored the team as well. My coaching colleague hosted multiple basketball camps for the city's kids that were staffed by the girls on the basketball team. These camps provided the girls with an opportunity to model alternative gender roles along with chances to talk about the importance of achieving academically and living responsibly. Finally, these camps provided an opportunity to learn and grow through service to others.

For the college athletes I worked with at the study center, deconstructing through sport took on an entirely different character. Most of these boys had learned through their schooling to view themselves as intellectually inferior and incapable of serious scholarship. While there was tremendous pride in their athletic exploits, there was a general lack of self-esteem when it came to academics. Several of these young men had been told as early as middle school not to worry about academics and one was given separate assignments from his peers. Another had his non-passing SAT scores published in several national magazines and newspapers. I once heard a television announcer mention his scores during a national broadcast.

At the university, these athletes had to contend with ridicule and hostility from classmates and instructors and an intensive time-consuming regimen on the playing field. Deconstructing sport for these young men meant learning to position themselves as both athletes and intellectuals. As they acquired the language of critique, they also gained awareness of the ways that their bodies were the property of the athletic department and its corporate sponsors. Most of them walked around with sponsored brands tattooed to their chests, legs, ankles, and feet.

Deconstructing through sport also meant acknowledging and then letting go of the harmful stereotypes that had shaped their young lives. Cultural theorist Henry Giroux describes the construction of youth identity in the corporate media. As high-profile athletes and as working-class males, these athletes were constructed as menacing, ignorant, overly sexualized, volatile, and unmotivated to succeed academically. For these college athletes, acquiring the tools and language of deconstruction precipitated a new reading of themselves and the world around them just as it had done for the high school girls' basketball players.

For some, this new reading contributed to the removal of corporate brands from their label-ridden flesh and the reclaiming of their bodies as their own texts. It also contributed to the development of subversive strategies to siphon time away from the sports program to redirect toward academic study. Many of these young men were able to take the first steps to reach out to those classmates and teachers who had shown them such hostility (except on football Saturdays, of course, when their detractors became screaming fans). For others, it led to fighting for the right to declare their own majors and not the ones "advised" for scholarship athletes. For others still, it led to fighting back against verbal abuse and demanding the right to be defined in one's own terms even if it meant suicide for the collegiate career, which it did for a few.

The deconstructing through sport also had a direct impact on the acquisition of academic literacy. Inspired by their work with the Athletic Study Center, the School of Education at this university created a Masters' Degree program for athletes who were interested in becoming teachers and coaches. The athletes who participated in this program sought to capitalize on the positive potential of sports participation while eliminating many of the abuses they had faced in their careers. Similar to the basketball program at North Bay High, they saw possibility of developing scholar athletes who excel in both athletics and academics while drawing upon lessons learned from the playing field to contribute to success in school and in life.

Considerations When Teaching Popular Sports

My first piece of advice for those teachers who are not coaches is to establish powerful relationships with the coaches at their schools. It is important for teachers to see coaches as allies rather than enemies. Honestly, teens are often more motivated to play for a particular coach than they are to complete the literacy tasks required in secondary classrooms. Also, there is considerable evidence that secondary students who participate in sports receive better grades and graduate at higher rates. For girls, there is a correlation between participation in sports and higher levels of self-esteem and lower rates of teen pregnancy.

Literacy educators can pitch the study hall idea to coaches and have coaches make suggestions for readings related to sports. Literacy teachers can also educate coaches and enable them to talk with their athletes about the connections with literacy practices associated with sports and academic literacy practices in secondary classrooms. English teachers can take the lead in helping students and coaches to regard athletic participation as an intellectual activity and one that is co-curricular and not tangential to the meaningful learning in schools.

At the same time, English teachers can facilitate critical dialogue about the relationship between sports and the greater society to help students come to critical readings of themselves as athletes, as consumers, and as citizens. At a time when identity development is such an important issue, these conversations can lead to more healthy attitudes and powerful writing products. The development of critical literacy entails not only a reading of the world but a re-writing of that world. These students can become catalysts in creating critical texts that are not only beneficial to them but are helpful to others as well.

I have tried to present a balanced view of participation in sports that reveals its benefits as well as its drawbacks. Whether sports participation is ultimately more helpful or harmful is not the primary issue here for English teachers. What's important is that adolescents are interested in or participating in sports in large numbers whether their teachers want them to or not. Sports participation also plays a major role in how young people view themselves, for better and worse I would argue. I am again taken back to a comment made by Giroux. Rather than holding popular culture in judgment, he argues, our task as critical educators is to recognize its centrality to the lives of youth and confront this culture in a sensitive and affirming, yet problematizing way. English teachers are perfectly positioned to draw upon youth participation in sports to develop competence and confidence in classroom literacy activities, while also developing the critical language that would enable these young women and men to become more empowered consumers and practitioners of sport.

Part Three
The Possibilities

Chapter 8

Preparing to Teach Popular Culture

Making the move toward incorporating popular culture necessitates a major change in the nature of knowledge consumption and production. In making this change, teachers are also expanding what counts as legitimate knowledge and challenging the notion that only certificated adults possess relevant knowledge. Finally, even though it is omnipresent, popular culture is elusive and ever-changing, depending on time and context. This differs from the literary canon, which is fairly bound and changes very slowly.

In response to these possible challenges and concerns, this chapter offers practical steps that all teachers can take to increase their confidence in using popular culture. Some suggestions are about changing or challenging existing attitudes and beliefs about popular culture, others are strategies for learning about popular culture and its participants. The chapter suggests how expert teachers who are popular cultural novices can plan and teach units incorporating popular culture as they learn from and with their students. It also begins to outline how teachers can learn as ethnographers of students' experiences with popular culture. Finally, this chapter makes recommendations for how teachers can access graduate programs and create or take advantage of professional development opportunities that will facilitate learning about popular culture.

Avoid Immediate Negative Judgment

My first piece of advice is for teachers to avoid immediate negative judgment of popular culture. Many of the pieces that will have the most positive impact on students are ones that teachers would not normally choose for themselves. Further, many may not consider these pieces classics or worthy of academic attention. I contend, though, that with the right attitude and preparation, these feelings will change. Within the discipline of English studies, these perceptions are already changing and any historical analysis of the discipline will reveal that works that began as popular (i.e., Shakespeare, Dickens, and so forth) or were marginalized (works by many women authors and authors of color) become canonical, showing that there is no pure and absolute distinction between what is "classic" and what is not. Usually, it is a question of timing, attitudes, and context. One major purpose of this book is to question and challenge attitudes that may unfairly limit the use of popular culture in educational contexts.

As teachers, it is important to believe in the students as sensible and thoughtful young people (bear with me). In other words, it is important to attempt to understand why certain elements of popular culture, such as films, television shows, songs, or magazines might be appealing to young people. The voyage of understanding and empathizing with students enough to make sense of their interests and out-of-school literacy practices will demand that teachers exit their comfort zone and see, as much as possible, through the eyes of the students. As this happens, there will certainly still be texts that seem unworthy or unacceptable and this is fine. Teachers, I argue shouldn't feel pressured to teach something that makes them uncomfortable; there are plenty of texts that will exist in the land of compromise and, in most cases, the students will be impressed that their teachers are even making the effort.

With that said, selection does play a major role here. Certainly, teachers will want to involve the students to some extent in the nomination and selection processes. Ultimately, though, the final decisions rest with the teacher. Just as one wouldn't casually walk into a bookstore and pick up any piece of fiction off the shelf to teach, one shouldn't haphazardly select works of popular culture. One of my students said it best several years ago that, "just as there are weak writers, there are weak emcees." The argument can be extended to other aspects of popular culture as well. In fact, it is safe to assume that, just as it is with fiction, only a few films, songs, or shows will be considered truly great and worthy of your time and the time of your students. Also, just as you would with fiction or poetry, your selection of popular cultural texts should consider theme, content, and age appropriateness. What would be a great novel for high school seniors might be too much for an eighth grade classroom. Similarly, a film that would be amazing for sixteen year olds might be too mature for eleven and twelve year olds.

I am confident, though, that avoiding immediate negative judgment will lead to the selection, indeed the discovery of some amazing texts that will blow you away. This will take effort, cooperation, and probably a steep learning curve initially, but it's worth it. There will undoubtedly be a host of students who will be able to help in this regard. When it comes to those final decisions, teachers should feel comfortable trusting their professional instincts in deciding what will fly. I would even recommend starting conservatively at first, especially if you feel uncomfortable or inexperienced around popular culture.

All I ask is that teachers give popular cultural texts the same consideration that they give to traditional texts. By this, I mean that teachers shouldn't be dismissive of potentially great texts that they see as problematic because of language, content, or theme. I hear many teachers dismiss genres of popular culture as violent, vulgar, or oppressive while they have no problem teaching classical texts like *Macbeth, Hamlet, The Sun Also Rises, The Great Gatsby*, and so on, texts that feature killing, adultery, fornication, excessive drinking, and racist and sexist language. I believe that teachers insist on these texts because they are powerful narratives of the awesome, yet flawed human condition. We do not necessarily celebrate the viewpoints and language that the authors use at all times, but we do celebrate the power of the narrative. There are even educators who introduce critical literary lenses such as feminism, Marxism, and postcolonialism to encourage students to read against these classical texts as evidences of problematic dominant narratives of society (Appleman, 2000). Again, I am only asking that popular cultural texts be given the same consideration and be treated in the same ways—as powerful, yet flawed portrayals of the human condition. I would even welcome teachers enabling students with critical literary lenses to apply to the popular culture that they consume. No one is arguing for a blind acceptance or celebration of popular culture; that would be dangerous and counterproductive. At the same time, however, having a higher bar for popular cultural texts than traditional texts is just not fair to the texts or to the students. A colleague of mine once said that if all the texts in the English department were treated like the popular cultural texts there would be nothing left to read. I tend to agree with her.

No One Is an "Expert" on Popular Culture

It is also important that teachers not feel as though they have to become experts on all elements of popular culture—no one is. I have heard teachers declare that they will begin teaching popular culture once they have mastered the content. There is so much content and it is so rapidly changing that the prospect is impossible. What's more important is that teachers acknowledge what they are experts of and what they are not. Even in a classroom, where the teacher does not have a mastery of the film text that the class is viewing, she or he still has expertise in curriculum design, assessment, student learning, leading discussions, writing instruction, and so on. It is important that teachers continue to feel valuable and necessary in classrooms that may focus on student-centered subject matter. Just because the students may have more experience with a particular genre or text doesn't mean that they no longer need a teacher to guide them, to generate assignments, to facilitate discussions, and to assess learning. On the contrary, such pedagogy requires even more of the teacher in my opinion.

At the same time, teachers can do a great deal to draw upon the expertise of the students while increasing their own expertise. Every teacher should have what I call student informants—that is, students who seem to have a great understanding of youth culture and a willingness to share their understanding with a teacher. The Brazilian critical educator Paulo Freire (1970) called this dynamic student-teachers and teacher-students. This is a powerful model for a classroom culture in which all have the opportunity to teach and learn. Again, for all of the reasons stated previously, this does not mean equality between teachers and students. What it does mean, though, is a respect for the students as knowledgeable subjects and co-creators of meaning in the classroom. These ideas are not new to critical education or to sociocultural theories of learning; they are the very foundation of constructivist conceptions of learning, which are foundational to contemporary educational psychology.

Though these ideas have been around for some time and are the staple of teacher credential programs and professional development seminars, I would argue that they are less prevalent in practice. Particularly rare is the idea of teachers and students sharing ownership of the sanctioned knowledge in the classroom. I can understand the many and varied reasons why this is difficult, if not nearly impossible, for many of us to do. I can say that I am in no way, shape, or form suggesting that teachers abnegate their responsibility as leaders and turn over their classrooms to the young people who desperately need them. I would also add that the possibilities for meaningful relationships between teachers and students and between students, texts, and the world may make the initial awkwardness and discomfort worthwhile.

Teachers as Ethnographers

One of the most important ways that teachers can learn about popular culture is to become ethnographers of the language and literacy practices of their students. Ethnography, a research tool developed by cultural anthropologists, is an approach to learning about the social and cultural life of communities, institutions, and other settings (LeCompte and Schensul, 1999, p.1). LeCompte and Schensul go on to say:

> Ethnography takes the position that human behavior and the ways in which people construct and make meaning of their worlds and their lives are highly variable and locally specific. One primary difference between ethnography as science and other social and behavioral science methods of investigation is that ethnography assumes that we must first discover what people actually do and the reasons they give for doing it before we can assign their actions interpretations drawn from our own personal experience or from our professional or academic disciplines. That is why the tools of ethnography are designed for discovery. (p. 1–2)

Geertz (2000) traces the evolution of anthropology, and in particular ethnography, from an initial focus on seeing the *other* as deficit or different to understanding the relationship between local knowledge and the human condition. The works of LeCompte and Schensul (1999) and Geertz all identify ethnography as an additive tool. That is, ethnography seeks to find and understand the logic and beauty of the practices of others that we may not initially understand; but if we are willing to suspend our own prejudices and beliefs, we may not only find out useful information about others, we may find that we better understand ourselves. As Geertz contends, it may be possible to find ourselves in the translation between cultures.

Of course, the idea of applying anthropological methods to educational contexts is nothing new. Many before have advocated that teachers learn from their students and their students' families. However, the advocacy has rarely been followed up by a discussion of the skills and tools that teachers need in order to learn from students and communities. Rarer still are examples of how teachers, as ethnographers, can learn from students and use this knowledge to transform classroom instruction. This book has set out to accomplish all of these tasks.

I know that this is a very difficult prospect for teachers to become ethnographers and to engage in ethnographies of language and literacy for a variety of valid reasons. Teachers that I have worked with in the past have been open to the idea but either feel that there isn't enough time or that they do not possess the skills to perform ethnographic investigations of the popular cultural practices of their students. With respect to the first concern, I can only suggest that the time used learning about students and the worlds they inhabit would be time well spent. All good teachers allot a certain percentage of their time to planning ahead or expanding their repertoires of content or disciplinary knowledge. Hopefully this text so far has made the argument that learning about students' interests and participation related to popular culture is a central part of relevant teacher knowledge. I would also add that teachers should not feel responsible to do all of the things that I suggest in this section. As time permits, simply follow a few of these suggestions and it should make a big difference. Several of the suggestions will not take any additional time out of the day and a few will only take minutes and not hours.

The most important skill that an ethnographer can possess is the ability to observe and record. Usually, ethnographers are charged with looking into the social world and noting customs, habits, and patterns that emerge from people's everyday activities—finding a form and purpose to the events that participants take for granted and do not think about. In other words, ethnographers can unpack or uncover cultural practices that are unknown, even to the participants. This is not to say that people cannot become ethnographers of their own cultural practices or that ethnographers are not participants in the sites that they study. I only mean to make the point that the primary role of an ethnographer is to find ways to make sense of what may be invisible to everyone else around.

As an ethnographer, you can begin to hone the skills of *participant observation* during the normal school day routine. On the trip to school, for example, an ethnographer of youth culture might pay particular attention to the advertising that is targeted toward the age group that she teaches. She or he may begin to ask questions and make notes of the latest films, music CDs, and television shows that find themselves plastered on billboards and bus stops or shop window displays. When on campus, this ethnographer might pay close attention to the scenery and conversations on the way to class. What are kids wearing? What are they talking about? What texts do they possess that relate to popular culture? This could include magazines, photos, compact discs, DVDs, or a host of others.

Once in the classroom, the teacher-ethnographer can continue the observations. What texts do the students bring into the classroom? What elements of popular culture do the students talk about on their way into and out of classroom? Teachers can also begin to discern which students are writers outside of the classroom as well. Are there any students in bands or in rap groups? Are there any aspiring filmmakers or screenwriters? How do they participate as textual consumers and producers via their involvement in these other activities?

When there is time, teacher-ethnographers can observe youth-dominated spaces in the surrounding community including parks and malls, convenience stores, even street corners. This is a perfect activity to assign pre-service teachers in a credential program or experienced teachers returning for a masters program (see Barton, 2000, and Moll, 2000). In these spaces, it is important to be considerate of the youth and not immediately judgmental of the practices. LeCompte and Schensul (1999) remind us that the first and primary task of an ethnographer is to observe and record, not to judge. Geertz (2000) would add that the important goal is not necessarily to get inside the minds of the participants, but to figure out, as much as possible, what it is they think they're up to (p. 58). An ethnographer of youth culture would be interested in the language and literacy practices of the youth in these particular settings and the meaning making that accompanied these practices. If it were a mall, she would want to pay attention to the places where the youth congregated, the activities associated with hanging in the mall, and the language and literacy practices associated with "Mall Hanging." For instance, she could watch young people in the music store to see how they use literacy to navigate this space making note of the texts they "read," whether jackets of CDs and DVDs or popular magazines. She can pay close attention to the critical or analytical skills the teens use when talking about these texts or when making selections among texts.

Ethnographers usually have notebooks where they record their observations, generally referred to as *field notes.* Field notes usually have two types of writing, observations and commentary. The most important determinant of quality field notes is the amount of thick description, which would fall under the category of observations. This would include as many specific details as possible. Only after recording details or description is commentary warranted. In this way, the training of an ethnographer prevents, as much as possible, premature evaluation of a particular context. Of course, all of this recording of thick description takes time. If teacher-ethnographers do not have time during the hectic schedule of the school day, they should try to make time immediately after school to record thoughts and observations. As a classroom teacher, I would try to find some time during my preparation period and a few moments before leaving for home to record significant observations about the school day. I have also gotten in the habit of always having a pen and a notebook when I am out and about in case I see something noteworthy to my continued investigations of youth and popular culture.

A second activity associated with ethnography is the collection of artifacts. Artifacts have been defined as the material products of human activity (Hodder, 1998). In your role as an ethnographer, some artifacts you might collect would be popular magazines, CDs, or DVDs. Certain magazines, such as *Billboard* and *Entertainment Weekly*, actually list the most popular books, compact discs, television shows, and movies in theatres. There is more information about sources of research on popular culture in Appendix J. A second source of artifacts could come from occasionally surfing the internet and "bookmarking" sites that are popular among or targeted toward adolescent users. An ethnographer might also videotape popular programs on television or even attend a movie in a theatre that is popular among students.

Other artifacts could include texts that students actually produce themselves such as lyrics, poems, plays, graffiti art, apparel, or demo tapes. Teachers may ask students to see examples of their poems, raps, or lyrics. They might also distribute surveys to ascertain youth interest and involvement in popular culture. At the beginning of the school year, for instance, the teacher-ethnographer might distribute a questionnaire to find out how often the students in the classroom access popular culture and in what forms. Such a simple instrument could yield important information regarding student interests, tastes, and practices associated with popular culture.

Finally, ethnographers use interviewing to obtain information from a population under study. There are different types of interviewing ranging from conversational to formal. There is also a difference from an individual interview to a focus group interview, which could involve a group of up to five or six individuals. There are plenty of chances in the normal school day to interview students about their engagement in popular culture. Given the intimate relationships between teachers and their students, these interviews would probably be on the informal side and would vary between individual and focus group. Teachers could ask students about the most popular shows, music, movies, styles of dress, or additions to youth language. They could query youth to determine what is going out of style or to comment on the changes in popular culture. Teachers could also ask students about the texts that they create in relation to their participation in the culture. Over time, there will probably emerge a small group of informants—or insiders—that the teacher can rely upon for accurate up to the minute information. At North Bay High, for instance, students, once learning of our interest in popular culture, would come into the classroom and make suggestions to us for music that we should buy or movies that we should attend. Some would even make copies of CDs for us to listen to and discuss with them.

Once teachers make the decision to incorporate popular culture into their curricula, the student informants will become invaluable. Teachers can ask these students about their opinions of the selections as well as for recommendations for future selections within a particular genre. As I have argued elsewhere, though, the final decisions should remain with the teacher. I do think, though, that there is a difference between using informants to learn about popular culture and having students offer advice on what texts might be used in classroom assignments. With respect to the latter, it is necessary that teachers move more slowly and more conservatively than they may want. With respect to the former, however, teacher-ethnographers should really try to make sense of the myriad student uses of popular culture, even, and maybe especially, those not deemed appropriate for classroom consumption. I always found it helpful to know how my students were interacting with popular culture, even when it may have been in problematic or self-defeating ways. I also found my perceptions of youth and youth-inspired texts challenged and enlightened by my conversations with insiders in the culture.

There are some excellent examples of ethnographies in language and literacy education for interested teachers and researchers. Luis Moll's "Ethnographies in Education" in Carol Lee and Peter Smagorinsky's *Vygotskian Perspectives in Literacy Research* (2000) describes a project in which pre-service teachers were required to enter the homes and communities of potential students to learn about the language practices and the local funds of knowledge contained there that could be drawn upon in classroom instruction. David Barton (2000), a researcher in Great Britain also has a project in which students were asked to enter neighborhoods and document the literacy events and literacy practices associated with everyday activity in those communities. Both Barton and Moll begin with the proposition that all people are learners and users of language and literacy as they participate in their everyday, sociocultural activity. This is a far cry from the attitudes of many schools, which see a large portion of their students as non-learners or non-literate. The perspectives that Barton and Moll encourage of their students is also the perspective that this book promotes. When teachers are able to identify the strengths and norms of their students, they can go a long way in teaching those students the concepts they need to succeed academically, socially, politically, and economically. Really, it is an idea as old as Vygotsky's (1978) concept of the Zone of Proximal Development. Vygotsky believed that expert practitioners are most successful in co-constructing knowledge when they begin with the learners' prior knowledge and experiences and gradually take them to a place where they could not have gotten without expert assistance.

For teachers interested in learning more about ethnography as a research method, there are cultural anthropologists who talk in more detail about many of the issues that I have laid out in this section. Clifford Geertz's (2000) essays in *Local Knowledge: Further Essays in Interpretive Anthropology* are excellent and well-written pieces for pre-service or practicing teachers who are seriously conducting ethnographic investigations of young people's language and literacy practices associated with participation in popular culture. Gumperz and Hymes's *Directions in Sociolinguistics: The Ethnography of Communication* (1986), and Hymes' *Reinventing Anthropology* (1999) are also excellent additions to any library of ethnographers of language and literacy. Finally, beginning books in cultural anthropology or qualitative research methods in education would be helpful. Generally, these books are quite readable for practitioners who may not have a great deal of experience with the language of social science research. Merriam's (1998) *Qualitative Research and Case Study Applications in Education* and Biklen and Bodkan's (1998) *Qualitative Research in Education* were invaluable to me as a classroom teacher attempting to engage in ethnographic research.

Appendix K contains a multitude of resources for the teacher-researcher, including further reading on the subject of ethnography. Though ethnography is a complex research tool that can be refined and perfected with training from experts, there are many activities that interested teachers can begin immediately without any additional guidance. Ultimately, however, I would argue that teachers attempt to create or participate in formal structures that will allow them to develop the tools they need to become ethnographers of students' cultures and proficient practitioners that are able to effectively incorporate popular culture in order to increase the literacy development of their students. It is toward two of these more formal structures, graduate education and professional development, that I now turn.

Learning About Popular Culture Through Graduate Coursework and Professional Development

I would strongly urge educators to create courses or mini-units within credential and Masters'-level programs that speak directly to ethnography. The benefits of such courses speak for themselves. This is especially relevant now at a time when increasing numbers of teachers are being required to return to school to acquire advanced certification. Too often, I know this was the case with my colleagues; teachers are forced to pursue general coursework in curriculum or instruction that does not necessarily meet the needs of any particular discipline. The alternative is to pursue an advanced degree in a particular discipline, such as English, that deals with esoteric content knowledge, usually literature and literary theory, outside of a context of teaching and learning. Departments of education can take proactive steps in creating programs that allow teachers to gain disciplinary knowledge, to learn more about teaching and learning in context, and that equip teachers with a set of methodological tools and strategies that they can use to learn more effectively about their students and the communities in which they live. All Master's programs that target practicing teachers should include courses and assignments that not only compel teachers to learn about their classroom practice, but also encourage teachers to learn about language and literacy learning in non-school contexts.

Practicing teachers can also be proactive in this process as well. When pursuing advanced education, teachers can become better consumers of programs locating the ones that offer them the most opportunities to learn and participate as teacher-researchers. Also, if programs do not offer the desired courses, teachers should make use of other departments on university campuses, such as English, film studies, ethnic studies, or anthropology, that offer more specific coursework related to their practice and goals.

Another important structure for formal learning includes professional development. Even for those teachers not planning to pursue advanced degrees, there is always the push for professional development. This usually takes several different forms. There is the whole-staff or whole-district professional development that involves outsiders coming into a site with knowledge; there are stipends and opportunities given to teachers to attend conferences or other educational settings; and there are also opportunities for a subset of teachers within a school or district to develop their own self-study plans or projects. Within all of these options, there are opportunities for individual teachers or coalitions to create opportunities to learn about popular culture.

If there is one complaint I had as a teacher or that I hear from practicing teachers, it is that professional development is usually boring and irrelevant. I see no reason why a group of teachers could not petition their principal or superintendent to bring in a specialist in popular culture, whether a practicing artist, a critic, or an educator with extensive experience in teaching popular culture to lead a professional development seminar. In my experience, I have come across numerous individuals who are qualified and willing to play such a role with teachers and districts. Few, if any, have been requested in such a capacity.

If teachers are unable to impact the school and district-wide professional development, there are regional and national conferences that they can attend and interact with practitioners and researchers who are using elements of popular culture in their work. Over the past decade, I have attended many such conferences around the country and I have seen a number of individuals present on such work. When perusing the conference bulletin, I encourage teachers to seek presentations that deal with music, film, media, sports, and youth culture in general. This is an excellent way to make connections with colleagues who share similar interests and to create meaningful learning communities that extend beyond the boundaries of the classroom. Once I began to attend and deliver these presentations myself, I gained many allies and I also gained many mentors who were able to stimulate my imagination of what was possible in my classroom.

Though the district-wide events and professional conferences can be excellent sources of information, I have written elsewhere (Morrell, 2003) that the most effective forms of professional development are unofficial learning communities that teachers create themselves. Sometimes these communities gain official sanction through a grant or some charge by an administrator, but just as often they form out of a need or desire and acquire a life of their own. I have come across such communities that have developed from mutual interests in teacher research and strategies for tapping into students' home cultures. I would advocate that teachers begin to seek out colleagues who are also interested in the possibilities of utilizing popular culture to create reading and discussion groups and, ultimately, collaborative research projects. At both North and South Bay high schools, I was lucky enough to participate in these collaborative groups; and, in each case, the learning communities were professionally stimulating.

The bottom line is that, though the process may be overwhelming, there are many opportunities for teachers who are willing to learn to become practitioners and researchers of popular culture. While I place a tremendous onus on departments of education to create relevant learning spaces, I believe that teachers can create their own spaces for learning, either individually or as members of collaborative communities. While a focal and primary source of learning about popular culture needs to be students and their communities, teachers also have a great deal to learn from popular cultural theorists, educational researchers, and, of course, their colleagues who are already involved in this revolutionary project. The immediate task for educators, then, is to locate the resources that will facilitate that necessary learning.

Chapter 9

Teaching Popular Culture in an Age of Standards and Censorship

Other valid concerns that I hear from teachers who may be interested in teaching popular culture (the first being addressed in chapter 8) are the lack of space in the curriculum given the current emphasis on standards and standardized tests and the threat of censoring from colleagues and administrators. I do not try to dismiss or minimize these very valid concerns. Rather, I attempt to provide information and strategies that may help to mitigate them in a way that does not compromise teachers' positions or the achievement goals of a particular school or school district.

One cannot open the newspaper or turn on the news without being bombarded with the supposed failure of America's schoolchildren. The proposed solutions to the "problem" of America's schools usually include some form of testing. Standardized tests, then, do far more than let teachers, students, and parents know how individual students are performing; they are the primary, if not sole indicators of school, district, state, and national academic performance. I have seen major newspaper columns that rank schools and districts based on test scores. Departments of education also rank schools and districts on their web sites. The results of low rankings can be devastating and range from reconstitution (firing or relocating all faculty and administrators in low-performing schools), lost resources, low morale, and even decreasing property values in the neighborhoods of low-performing schools.

It's no wonder then, that student learning and academic achievement are being increasingly tied to standardized test scores, as opposed to other traditional, more localized teacher assessments of student work. Indeed, as I have traveled around the country and spoken with teachers, and visited classrooms and schools, I can definitely feel an increased sense of anxiety and urgency surrounding standardized tests and their consequences. The primary complaint of the teachers I talk to is that their curricula are being reduced and prescribed to produce better test-takers, and not necessarily better learners and users of language and literacy in the ways the teachers feel are valuable. I want to make the case that this does not have to be an either/or proposition; it is possible to have curricula that help students perform on standard measures without having to throw out innovative ideas to teach to the test. In fact, I would argue that the teachers and the schools that have the most anxiety over performance on standardized tests are also the ones that stand to benefit the most from the practices suggested in this book.

It is unfortunate that innovative curricula, particularly curricula that focus on issues of multiculturalism, diversity, or social critique, have been labeled as inherently soft, non-rigorous, or counterproductive to the goals of increasing academic achievement. Further, approaches to teaching that are more student- or activity-centered are also seen as easy or lightweight. By contrast, classical texts and traditional methods of instruction are deemed the only pathways to helping "students" to acquire the skills that they need to pass the batteries of tests that are annually levied upon them. I place students in quotes because these reforms are generally targeted toward a certain subset of the student population, usually the population that is already most alienated and victimized by the school system and society at large.

This is not to say that standards aren't important or that students, teachers, and administrators should not be held accountable for learning outcomes. While I do feel that students, parents, and teachers bear an unfair amount of accountability for circumstances that are usually beyond their control, I certainly agree that students need to learn the skills necessary to integrate into a modern society that demands increasingly higher levels of literacy from its citizens and workers. However, I take serious issue with the idea that the only way to address the current standards is to revert to texts and approaches that have really never been successful with the students who are the targets of current educational reform.

This chapter acknowledges, even accommodates, the recent focus at the state and national levels, on standardized tests as the primary evaluator of academic achievement. Within this context, the chapter provides a framework for literacy educators to envision a practice of the teaching of popular culture that is commensurate with the current educational climate while also meeting various other goals such as being culturally and socially relevant (Ladson-Billings, 1994) and preparing students for their roles as participants in and residents of the global village. Further, this chapter makes the case that literacy educators should be at the forefront of conversations about alternate forms of assessing students' literacy levels that are more compatible with recent developments in literacy studies and inclusive of students' non-school literacy practices, such as those associated with participation in popular culture.

The second portion of the chapter deals with the questions surrounding popular culture and censorship. Numerous teachers who are excited about the possibilities of teaching popular culture have worries about being censored by their colleagues and administrators. Again, these concerns are warranted as popular culture has a somewhat justified, though largely unfair reputation as a corrupting influence on the young and the innocent. In this chapter, I take a cultural-historical approach to the perceptions toward popular culture in society that outlines many of the inherent prejudices in the distinctions made between canonical and popular culture while also giving teachers a set of strategies that may make it easier to begin to include elements of popular culture alongside their more traditional offerings.

Popular Culture, Standards, and Standardized Tests

First, it is important to define what we mean by standards for adolescent literacy in the English language arts. To do this, I have looked at the most recent standards published by the National Council of Teachers of English and the International Reading Association. I have also examined papers on adolescent literacy commissioned by the Carnegie Foundation and the National Reading Conference to contribute to the understanding of what needs to be happening in quality secondary English classrooms. Despite some minor differences, there is a general consensus between the International Reading Association, the National Council of Teachers of English, the National Reading Conference, and the state-level standards in California and Michigan (the two states where I have the most experience) on what constitutes a quality secondary English curriculum. All of these standards encourage classrooms where students encounter wide ranges of print and literature, learn to respect diversity in languages and cultures, employ a variety of comprehension strategies, participate in the writing process, and gain an understanding of technology to facilitate the literacy learning process.

In my experience as a teacher and teacher educator who advocates the use of popular culture, I have rarely seen any inconsistency between the curricular approaches I advocated or any of the state and national standards that I encountered. To the contrary, I have found that the most important consideration for teachers who use innovative or unique approaches is to communicate how a particular lesson plan adheres to department, district, or state standards. In my teacher education classes I would have students explicitly demonstrate how their lessons were responding to standards. In my own letters to parents and in communications with administrators, I always spoke of my curriculum in relationship to the standards we were held to at that particular moment. This wasn't particularly a challenge because, with respect to the standards, my goals were the same as the majority of my colleagues and superiors who also wanted all students to receive a quality, rigorous, and relevant curriculum. Even when the district mandated certain texts, I was able to create thematic units that I supplemented with popular cultural texts.

Indeed, I stand by the examples provided in chapters 4 through 7 as evidence of rigorous and relevant curricula that included the study of popular culture. As long as teachers are open and explicit in making connections between their units and the standards, potential problems are minimized because, in general, standards are documents created by teachers to ensure a quality of instruction that still allows teachers a sense of autonomy and creativity to achieve mandated outcomes.

It is important to state, however, that standards and standardized tests are two different entities entirely. In fact, it is often the case that standards are incompatible with standardized tests. As opposed to standards, tests are rarely created by teachers and even less likely to be scored by teachers. Rather than serving as formative assessments of the process of learning, standardized tests are summative assessments that are more evaluative in nature. Students don't usually receive their test scores, usually numbers, or percentile rankings, until months after taking the tests when they are in different classes, if not different grade levels.

This book recognizes, though, that teachers are bound and obligated by both standards and standardized tests. In many ways, the standardized tests have preeminence given that they are tied to funding, performance evaluations, and in some cases, even termination of employment or reconstitution of schools, and takeovers of entire districts. While I have made the case for the coordinated relationship between curriculum and standards, the connection between this approach and success on standardized tests is more complex. At the same time, it is important to consider how to help students be more successful on standardized tests even while being critical of these tests, their origins, and their ultimate purposes.

I would like to begin by offering a brief historical sketch of the development and functioning of standardized tests before discussing strategies educators might use to navigate these tests, pointing out how popular culture may aid in this process. My point is not to trash these tests; in the immediate future, personal feelings about standardized tests are inconsequential to the need to prepare students to perform on them. I do, however, believe that background information is important for educators to communicate with colleagues, parents, and students in attempts to preserve teacher autonomy and spaces for curricular innovation in a time of high-stakes testing.

The Ascendancy of Standardized Tests

David Tyack and Larry Cuban, authors of *Tinkering Toward Utopia: A Century of Public School Reform* (1995) correlate the ascendancy of standardization and standardized tests in the 1970s and 1980s to growing concerns about decreasing quality in education in the post-Brown era of schooling. Cuban and Tyack argue that the more "nontraditional" students gained access to secondary and post-secondary schooling, the more concerns grew about the quality of education in the nation. In fact, the authors contend, there has been an ongoing tension between equality and quality; that is, to the extent that education tends toward equality of access and inclusion, there are concerns about overall quality. Tyack and Cuban argue that the standardization movement of the 1970s and 1980s did a great deal to undo the equity gains of the 1950s and 1960s.

Even today, the primary focus of standardized tests has been to target poor children and children of color and the schools that serve them. As Tyack and Cuban point out, these tests are rarely used to champion students and schools. In fact, the opposite is far more often the case. The reporting of test scores is a time to bemoan the state of schools and students, generally poor and minority students. In a recent issue of *Time*, the major focus pertained to the failures of urban education as evidenced primarily by scores on standardized tests.

Cohen and Neufield (1981) point toward the competing goals of schooling as the source of conflict that results in a climate of over-emphasis on testing and achievement. These authors identify schools as the primary if not the sole social institution in the United States seriously concerned with issues of equality. At the same time, how-ever, schools and the public that accesses them, are influenced by, and subjected to larger market forces. That means that any increase in access for students who have been historically marginalized mini-mizes competitive advantage. It also means that in a world of scarce resources, there necessarily need to be mechanisms to determine who gets access to those scarce resources. After all, everyone can't go to Harvard, so there needs to be some way, such as testing, to sort out the winners from the losers.

The testing as sorting logic certainly resonates with my experi-ences as an educator. In California, where students and schools are assigned percentile rankings, I often wonder how there could ever truly be improvement. There would always be schools in the 90th percentile and the 10th percentile. North Bay High, which was al-ways closer to the 10th percentile than the 90th, was generally ridi-culed once the annual scores were released. There was no directive for improvement; the tests didn't really tell us much more about ourselves than the numbers documented in the school paper. It was difficult for me to find an uplifting, inspiring, or even pedagogical reason for having the tests and making the results public. I could only imagine how my students felt about the public scrutiny.

The historical foundations articulated by Tyack and Cuban (1995) and by Cohen and Neufield (1981) are important for teachers who find themselves in the middle of the storm. It is important to under-stand that the current ascendancy of tests had a beginning date and initial purpose that can still be identified a generation later. Under-standing the social and political purposes of the testing craze, I ar-gue, can embolden teachers to take many of the steps that I advocate later in this chapter.

The Educational Costs of Standardized Tests

Linda McNeil, in her book *Contradictions of School Reform: The Educational Costs of Standardized Testing* (2000) makes two key arguments that result from her multi-school study in Texas:

1. Standardization reduces the quality and quantity of what is taught and learned in schools; and

2. Over the long term, standardization creates inequities, widening the gap between the quality of education for poor and minority youth and that of more privileged students. (p. 3)

McNeil found that once the state bureaucracy began to centralize curriculum and promote tests and accountability as a reform strategy, the quality of teaching and learning suffered in the schools she studied. Teachers were less able to bring their personal and professional knowledge into the classroom as they were compelled to engage in what McNeil termed defensive teaching, or the shifting away from autonomous intellectual activity to the dissemination of packaged fragments of information mandated by upper-level bureaucracy. The teaching practices McNeil observed were circumscribed by the need for compliance, the need to cover generic curriculum, and the need to conform to knowledge as it is presented on centralized tests.

One of the contradictions that McNeil uncovers is the widening gulf between academic standards and the content to which students are exposed under a highly centralized system of standardized testing. McNeil documents cases of teachers taking away time normally devoted to reading and discussing literature to instead engage in rote memorization or to cover test preparation materials.

McNeil found that the climate of high-stakes testing and central control demoralized schools and separated the public and practitioners from school policy. Principals became agents of the state bureaucracy rather than leaders who are responsible to the needs of teachers, students, and communities. Further, the climate limited discourse on the nature and purpose of schooling while masking larger structural inequities in the name of accountability.

The Stereotype Threat and Standardized Tests

It is important for literacy educators to understand that there is not an absolute correlation between the development of academic skills and standardized test scores. There are a host of other factors that can affect student performance. Claude Steele, a Stanford-based psychologist, has conducted numerous experiments that have confirmed the existence of the stereotype threat. That is, when students feel that they are being judged as members of a stereotyped group rather than as individuals, they do worse on tests. In Steele's (2003) experiments, the stereotype threat applied to students of color on standardized tests and among women in mathematics when gender stereotypes operate.

It can be argued that these same stereotypes are present for students of color and students who attend historically underperforming schools. I have already mentioned how these schools are singled out in local newspapers that students and their families have to read. I have also seen schools hold rallies that are meant to motivate students to perform well, but actually end up reaffirming students' perceptions of themselves as inferior. It is obvious that the overt and negative attention from the often well-intentioned media and school administration can have a negative impact on students' psyches when they take high-stakes tests.

This is not to suggest that nothing can be done to improve students' abilities to perform on standardized tests. Certainly there is some connection between academic literacy and test scores; so curricula that promote literacy skills, such as those mentioned in this book, can also improve students' scores on standardized tests.

What's more important about these innovative curricula are that they allow teachers to express creativity while giving students confidence in their abilities as literacy learners. Hilliard (2003) visited a number of schools across the country where historically underperforming students were achieving at high levels. Two common components of these successful schools included spaces for teachers to be creative and environments that promoted confidence among students.

This certainly makes sense; when teachers, through their curriculum and instruction, are able to communicate to students that they have confidence in them and that they are capable of achieving at high levels, this confidence can translate into higher performance on tests. Rather than being stereotyped for failure, an innovative and affirming curriculum can tell students that they are prepared to perform in ways that a monotonous drill-and-kill approach cannot.

The critical teaching of popular culture gives students a positive sense of themselves as members of vibrant cultural communities. Part of the stereotype threat stems from students not receiving affirming messages about themselves as cultured, gendered beings.

An empowering pedagogy that allows students to develop a sense of themselves as individuals and members of diverse cultures can mitigate some of the negative effects of larger social stereotypes.

Finally, a critical approach to teaching that includes the study of popular culture can open up spaces for teachers and students to have meaningful, substantive conversations about the nature of standardized tests. I have found that once students were able to talk openly about the tests and their feelings, they were more willing to confront the tests, even if they were still nervous and anxious about having to do so. These critical spaces also allowed students to feel as if they were working together against a common foe instead of competing against one another. Finally, with their work from the course, students had other indicators of their ability that they could juxtapose against their percentile rankings on standardized tests.

The bottom line is that, although they may be necessary, standardized tests in their current configuration are extremely problematic. Schools that are grossly under-funded and under-resourced must compete on supposed equal footing with the most wealthy and highly resourced schools. The least empowered participants, teachers and students, are often left taking the blame for larger structural inequities that are largely beyond their control. It makes sense for teachers, parents, and community members to contend against the misuse and overuse of these tests and their social, cultural, psychological, and educational outcomes.

That being the case, there are still actions that individual teachers and students can take to more effectively navigate these tests. Most paramount, teachers can work to retain autonomy as they develop lessons that instill confidence and voice to their students while opening up spaces for dialogue about standardized tests and the world that administers them. Also, as with censorship, it is important for teachers to develop a language to explain seemingly subversive and radical decisions to students, parents, colleagues, and superiors.

On Censorship

It is virtually impossible to talk about popular culture these days without talking about censorship. While I would argue that this has more to do with perceptions of popular culture than its actual content, the reality is not one to take lightly. For this reason, the remainder of the chapter deals with this issue of censorship and the teaching of popular culture. I begin by offering competing definitions of art to establish a cultural-historical perspective of the negative attitudes toward popular culture by practitioners within the academy. It seems that texts designated as "legitimate art" have far more leeway in being deemed appropriate for secondary curricula despite dealing with adult themes, containing adult language, and containing violence, xenophobia, and misogynistic ideals. I next explore the relationship between art and life in making the argument that popular and classical texts are important because they do illuminate life, even those facets of our existence that we would rather not see. I conclude with an initial discussion of the politics of teaching popular culture sharing my own experiences as a teacher and as one who has heard the stories of countless other teachers who have made the decision to teach popular culture in their classrooms.

What is Art?

This question has captured the imaginations of theorists, critics, philosophers, and lay persons for the course of human history. If the debates teach anything, it is that art is culturally defined and that definitions are subjective and dependent on time, place, and perspective. For example, many genres and art forms that were considered base or crude to contemporaries have risen to the level of art in successive generations. Take, for example, the work of Shakespeare, Dickens, Joyce, or the Beat writers. Other examples include ordinary artifacts that were used generations ago for everyday purposes that now litter our art museums and auction for millions of dollars.

During most of the twentieth century, this debate has manifested itself in the distinctions between high art and popular culture. Older, more traditional art forms such as opera and literature were elevated to the status of elite while the products of television, film, radio, and popular media were denigrated as the art of the "common man." Cultural theorists going as far back as Raymond Williams, Stuart Hall, and the work of the Birmingham Centre for Contemporary Cultural Studies have argued for an elimination of this distinction. Recently, there has been a blurring of these distinctions, especially with film and contemporary music, with the proliferation of film and jazz festivals and literary societies devoted to the study and celebration of these art forms. In secondary schools, however, little has changed within the last 50 years regarding which genres of texts are deemed acceptable for literary study.

In secondary English classrooms, those works labeled as classical or literary often have more freedom with respect to content or theme. Given that these works are, first and foremost, art, there is a certain understanding and tolerance for troubling depictions, outmoded language, and sensitive, mature themes. Texts laden with racial slurs, profanity, rape, violence, murders, suicides, homophobia, and the objectification of women are paraded through English courses and even featured on Advanced Placement reading lists with little or no problems from teachers, administrators, or parents who hold them in high esteem as literary classics.

I am not disagreeing with this practice in the slightest; I feel that many of the most powerful works that speak to today's youth from across the generations contain mature and offensive elements. I only bemoan the fact that other, equally worthy texts not so canonized are picked apart and left out for contradictory reasons. These works, among them films, musical selections, magazine articles, and videogames, are not seen as art. Language, mature references, racism, and sexism are not tolerated in the name of art as with the classics. Instead, school districts label these texts as vulgar and unimaginative and prevent their inclusion among more serious curricular selections. Such conflicting reasoning makes it difficult for teachers to make compelling cases for the inclusion of controversial popular texts into secondary curricula.

Art is Life

In her groundbreaking work of African American literary criticism *Playing in the Dark: Whiteness and the Literary Imagination*, author Toni Morrison (1993) asserts that national literatures reflect what is on the national mind. This is an important concept to consider when determining the worthiness and relevance of particular popular cultural texts for classroom instruction. Many of the problematic, disempowering, and deficit portrayals of characters based on their race, ethnicity, language, gender, socioeconomic status, or sexual identity stem from problematic representations of these groups in society. If students are indeed to learn more about themselves as situated socially, historically, and culturally from their reading of literature, then they need to be exposed to that national psyche, for better and for worse.

I advocate that teachers use critical literary theories such as Marxism, feminism, and postcolonialism to approach classical and popular texts in ways that enable students that represent groups which are marginalized in these texts and to help all students learn

about the power of texts to affirm or degrade those who are classi-
fied as "selves" or "others" in these texts. If art is indeed life, or is at
least inspired by life, then teachers need to confront and challenge
literary works that reflect problematic aspects of life rather than
promote approaches that defer to the wisdom or superiority of the
author. At the same time, it sends a disempowering message to students to challenge the limited thinking apparent in popular works
while implicitly exonerating classical texts that feature this same
thinking.

The Politics of Teaching Popular Culture

Teachers should not teach any texts that they are uncomfortable
with. There are plenty of worthy popular cultural texts that are not
going to set off fireworks with departmental colleagues or administrators. By the same token, however, I challenge colleagues to be
articulate about what they mean by inappropriate when they apply
this descriptor to popular texts. In the discipline of secondary English, Advanced Placement students have the privilege of reading
texts such as Allen Ginsberg's "Howl" or Toni Morrison's *Beloved*
when popular texts of similar themes or content are denigrated. In
my senior English classes, for instance, the most violent and "im-
moral" texts of the course were Shakespeare's *Hamlet*, *Othello*, and
Macbeth with their litany of betrayals, murders, and suicides.

As the discipline of English studies is continually defined, English teachers are challenged to entertain questions about what constitutes art and literature. In the course of their teaching, they are
frequently asked to supply rationales for texts that are not part of
the mainstream curricula. At major universities, there is much less
debate when it comes to the relationship between popular culture
and academic study. Students attending the most elite universities
have multiple course offerings in film and media studies as part of
their English majors. For example, at Columbia University, English
majors are required to take a course in drama or film and the department features offerings such as Film Noir and 20th Century Film.
At Michigan State University, where I now teach, the English department offers a concentration in Film Studies as well. Literary
critics, for a generation, have gleaned material from popular film,
music, and television for their analyses. The acceptance of popular
cultural art forms in higher education and literary circles places in
serious question the motives of opponents of teaching popular culture in secondary classrooms, especially if the goals of secondary

education are to prepare youth for college-level work and for their life as citizens.

Of course, this does not preclude the importance of communicating with parents about the objectives and content of the courses their children are taking. I believe that it is possible to be explicit, but not apologetic about including popular culture in the curriculum. Each year, colleagues and I would send a letter to parents letting them know that several course selections, including popular and canonical texts, would deal with mature themes and possibly feature "mature" language (excuse the euphemism; no one uses so-called mature language more than young people). The introductory letter explained the rationale for these selections, but also gave parents the right to withhold their children from participation in any unit with no consequence to the child's grade. The letters, which were sent out with the syllabus on the first day, were to be signed and returned and kept on file.

I would still like to underscore that the popular selections for my courses rarely, if ever, featured excessive violence, foul language, or sexual situations. I contend emphatically that there are so many quality texts available that do not stir the flames of controversy that it is hardly worth the battle to include the texts that do. However, there may occasionally be a text worth the trouble and I encourage teachers to stand up for their beliefs. Colleagues from past and present have fought diligently for the right to teach powerful and provocative contemporary texts such as *Catcher in the Rye*, *Catch-22*, *The Bluest Eye*, *Neuromancer*, and "Howl" I would argue that the discipline is stronger for these inclusions. The discipline of English studies will be stronger still at the secondary level when curricula regularly include a wide range of popular media selections.

If a general theme has emerged over this chapter, it is that teachers, in order to preserve ownership and creativity in their classrooms, may need to become activists and advocates. Many of the most innovative and most effective strategies for teaching today's youth will require practitioners with the willingness to contest against existing norms within the discipline and within educational policy. I started the first chapter by issuing a challenge to literacy educators; while it may not be easy, meeting the challenge and transforming the discipline are not impossible either. Standardization and censorship are serious issues that affect all literacy educators today. I have tried to present an approach to standardization and censorship that is critical, without being irreverent. I certainly understand why state and national governments need to keep abreast of how students and schools are performing. I also understand why departments, schools, and districts need to keep a close watch on the texts and ideals to which young people are exposed. I also believe, however, that there are no neutral decisions, that every educational choice, from policy to curriculum and instruction, has larger political outcomes. Some of the negative outcomes associated with standardized tests and censorship include limited opportunities for teachers and students to work together within innovative curricula that motivate students to greatness and lead to the kind of achievement that we know is possible with all students, not just a select few. If students are being denied access to excellent education because of current policies and practices, then that is a problem that needs to be addressed by the practitioners dedicated to providing that excellent education.

In the final chapter, I will issue one further challenge. Not only do teachers need to position themselves as advocates and activists, but they also need to document and share these experiences by publishing their work. The sleeping giant within the educational discourse at present are the two and a half million teachers with powerful stories of classroom practice and amazing potential as educational advocates. After reading this book, I hope that many are encouraged to write their own stories as part of becoming architects of the future of the discipline and the future of education.

Chapter 10

Teachers as Activists and Researchers

Hopefully, I have made many of these points by now but, given the summative nature of conclusions, some repetition is warranted. Certainly teaching popular culture calls for a reconsideration of the curriculum and methods of instruction in secondary English classrooms. I begin this chapter, however, with an explanation of how popular cultural texts can exist alongside more canonical works in rich multigenre curricular units that draw from the strength of both. The final sections, then, expand upon the idea of teachers as action researchers and political agents. The next section focuses on teachers as activists and advocates for curricular change in America's schools. It draws upon the work of Henry Giroux and others who have claimed that the teaching profession is increasingly mechanized with teachers having less and less say in the day to day composition of their lessons. Giroux (1988) calls for teachers, as public intellectuals, to resist these processes and to work collectively to transform them. The third section looks toward a burgeoning movement, practitioner research, which offers a pathway for teachers to function as public intellectuals while providing the teacher knowledge that can transform the discipline. In this section, I outline the emerging tradition of practitioner research focusing specifically on the action research and critical research traditions. I identify key proponents of these traditions, the core tenets of each, the implicit and explicit challenges of each, and the potential of each to transform the research process and, ultimately, classroom practice.

The final section makes a call to action for more teachers to become textual producers and action researchers who investigate, with their students, the multiple outcomes associated with innovative classroom practices and create texts to share with colleagues, parents, administrators, professional organizations, and policymakers on the importance of generating new approaches to the teaching of English/language arts in new century American schools. I am simultaneously arguing for practitioner-originated research that not only allows teachers the space to take ownership over the enterprise of knowledge production in their own profession but that also encourages teachers to become critical researchers who work with students, parents, and community members in larger struggles that are geared toward self- and social emancipation.

Popular Cultural Texts and Canonical Texts

It is unfortunate that much of the original backlash against the teaching of popular culture stems from a perception that all canonical or classical texts are to be purged from the curriculum. Nothing, in my estimation, could be further from the truth. I have advocated consistently throughout this book and in earlier research that popular cultural texts and classical texts function side by side in rich multigenre curricula that introduce students to thematic similarities between the texts of their own time and the texts of past cultures or distant places (Morrell and Duncan-Andrade, 2002). For example, the Poet in Society unit featured in chapter 4 has students comparing contemporary hip-hop texts with classical and canonical poets such as Shakespeare, John Donne, T.S. Eliot, and Maya Angelou. Similarly, the film units in chapter 5 also feature classical and modern texts such as *The Odyssey* and *Native Son*. While I might argue that the literary canon needs to be expanded, I would not argue for its dissolution. Classical texts are "classic" for a reason. Often, they reveal a great deal about who and what we have been historically and allow us to think about universals in the human condition. A truly thorough and representative literary canon can go a long way toward helping students and teachers to appreciate the wonderful diversity and amazing similarities among the human condition across time and space.

It is possible, even desirable, for teachers to conceive of multigenre or multimedia units that are arranged thematically instead of chronologically for a particular literary period or geographical region. For example, in my teacher education courses at Michigan State University, I have the pre-service teachers prepare multimedia units that must include: (1) novel or play; (2) film or television show episode; (3) poems; (4) popular songs; and (5) magazines, newspaper clippings, and so on. Some examples of themes we have used include:

1. Justice/Equality/Diversity
2. The American Dream
3. Coming of Age
4. The Triumph of the Human Spirit
5. Beauty and Society

Teachers can co-plan a series of thematically based, multimedia units that draw upon classical, modern, and popular cultural texts in a similar way to the assignments I have created for my prospective teachers enrolled in our credential program. It is easy to see how five or six of these integrated units could encompass an entire year-long course and allow teachers to meet district and state curriculum mandates while also providing opportunities for students to interact with multiple genres of popular cultural texts.

I must, however, warn against the tendency to use the popular texts in these multimedia texts as "bridge" texts or jumping off points into the more rigorous and intellectually stimulating classical work. Unfortunately, some of my earlier writing on teaching popular culture can fall into this category, even though it was never my intent. I say unfortunately, because such an approach can reinforce some of the deficit assumptions about the young people and traditional academic content that this book is trying to address. Moreover, such an idea is completely inaccurate. Students, as I have hopefully shown, are able to engage popular texts to derive complex analyses just as they can with any traditional or classical text. One only need peruse the latest doctoral dissertations flowing out of English departments to gain a sense of the intellectual activity surrounding the critical consumption of popular culture.

This book is heavily indebted to the work of Vygotsky and Vygotsky-inspired cultural-historical psychology that encourages teachers to draw upon the everyday experiences of young people to teach them complex academic concepts through engagement in meaningful sociocultural activity (Cole, 1996; Lee and Smagorinsky, 2000; Moll, 2000; Rogoff, 1990). However, I do not agree with Vygotsky that this movement through a Zone of Proximal Development is one from the simple to the complex. Rather, I see the movement as one from the familiar to the unfamiliar. It is also important to conceive that the critical tools made available through superior

English instruction will make the familiar strange to students as they learn to decode their own cultural practices with new language and it will also make the strange familiar as they understand the relationships between contemporary cultural texts and classical ones. Similarly, teachers who are also impacted from the work of cultural-historical psychology should not view the relationship between popular culture and canonical literature as a hierarchy or a journey from the simple to the complex. Rather, they should view this association as a series of conversations with students' immediate worlds and the varied words and worlds of literature. It is within this conceptual language that I offer the final comments of this text.

Teachers as Activists and Intellectuals

Though I have spent much of the last few chapters making the case for how teachers can function within the current school system, I also want to contend that teachers need to be leaders in contesting against the exclusionary and limiting practices in schools and classrooms while also working to re-articulate and refine the discipline at the secondary level. I have come across many teachers who feel that the only way to realize the potential of students is to substantially restructure the system of schooling. This project, though, requires a dual approach from English teachers who must navigate and work within the system while also working to change it.

Many theorists and researchers (Aronowitz and Giroux, 1991; Freire, 1997; Giroux, 1988; hooks, 1994; McLaren, 1994) have described the current process of deskilling teachers—where "teacher-proof curricula" and pacing guides limit the creativity and independent decision making of individual teachers. Within this climate, it becomes increasingly difficult for teachers to function as activists and intellectuals even though that is what is needed most. Teachers who do speak out against standard practices are seen as troublemakers when such activity is rewarded, even demanded in other professions. I was in a meeting not long ago where teachers were compared (as they always are) with the professions of medicine and law. One participant spoke out saying that a major difference between medicine, law, and education was that doctors and lawyers had a great deal more control over their professional practices than did teachers, who were largely beholden to administrators and policy makers to determine the nature of curriculum and instruction. This final chapter is part of a direct attempt to argue for how teachers can begin to regain some of that ownership over the discipline and of the schools in which they teach.

I grant that the situation is bleak, but not impossible. I urge educators to continue to struggle for changes that lead to more humanizing socially and culturally relevant curricula and the increased development of literacies of power. Educators should not be deterred by seemingly pejorative labels such as "political" or "ideological" understanding that there is no teaching practice that is not political and ideological (Apple, 1990). To continue to offer instruction that preserves an inequitable status quo is a political act. Rather than ask whether politics are reflected in practice, English teachers need to constantly consider how political views are reflected in practice as they strive to uncover contradictions between stated political or philosophical views on teaching and the realities of classroom practice. The backdrops to such reflections are, at once, the harsh realities of America's literacy classrooms juxtaposed against the tremendous potential for student learning and social transformation as presented in chapters 4 through 7 of this book.

On a related note, I also argue that teachers need to position themselves as public, transformative intellectuals (Giroux, 1988; Gramsci, 1971). What I mean by this is that teachers need to insert themselves into public conversations and debates about educational reform. While most people are hesitant to label themselves experts or intellectuals, teachers do have important perspectives and experiences that are absent from public conversations on educational matters. Teachers that are equipped with a combination of theory, research, and practical experience should be at the forefront of discussions about the nature of public education.

As public intellectuals, teachers need to speak out at board meetings, write to local officials, contribute editorials to newspapers, and offer commentary on radio shows. Certainly, teachers are not welcome participants in all of these forums, but I believe that we sometimes underestimate and underutilize our rhetorical power and ability to manipulate public forums and insert ourselves into important conversations. Because of the central position in the educational process, it is difficult to silence or dismiss teachers who are able to cull data, theory, and experience in provocative ways. It is because of this potential power that I want to speak at length about the necessity of teachers becoming critical researchers and textual producers.

Teachers as Critical Researchers
and Textual Producers

For well over a decade, there has been substantial attention paid to the importance of teacher research in educational reform (Cochran-Smith & Lytle, 1993; Smith and Stock, 2003; Zeichner and Noffke, 2001). I want to acknowledge this literature while also advocating for teachers to become critical researchers who engage in collaborative inquiry with students intended to challenge practices, discourses, and texts for the purpose of literacy learning and self- and social transformation.

Just what is meant by critical research and how is it different from research as it is traditionally conceived? At the risk of drawing an arbitrarily simple dichotomy, traditional research is usually defined by objectivity, by distance between researcher and researched, and the generalizability of results. These traditional notions of research are implicitly critical of teacher research and have been invoked to speak against the rigor or value of teacher research projects and the genre of practitioner research in general.

This is not to discount or discredit traditional research as having no relevance to contemporary issues in language and literacy education. Literacy research conducted by anthropologists, psychologists, sociologists, linguists, and educational researchers is invaluable to the field. I encourage teachers to become critical consumers of more traditional research as well, which breaks with the stereotypes of teachers being unwilling or unable to navigate academic texts. There is much within the academic research tradition that teachers need to consider and incorporate into their practice. Of course, there is also much that traditional research leaves out, most notably research accounts written from the perspectives of involved and interested participants such as teachers and students.

My preference would be to have multiple accounts of action research and critical research sit alongside more traditional research studies in teacher education programs and professional development seminars. For example, texts such as Jeffrey Wilhelm's *You Gotta BE the Book: Teaching Engaged and Reflective Reading With Adolescents* (1997) and Carol Lee's *Signifying as a Scaffold for Literary Interpretation: The Pedagogical Implications of an African American Discourse Genre* (1992) have been invaluable to my work as a teacher, a researcher, and a teacher educator. Wilhelm studied creative strategies, such as the incorporation of informal drama activities, to get reluctant readers more involved in classroom texts. Lee studied various units that she taught in English classrooms in Southside Chicago where she drew upon African American students' language practices to teach literary interpretation. The Wilhelm and Lee studies, both conducted from the perspectives of classroom teachers, have changed the way that literacy educators think about secondary reading and literature instruction. Each study does an excellent job of combining complex theories (such as reader-response theories or sociocultural psychology) with classroom practices in a manner that is both grounded and accessible. Without drawing upon these theoretical perspectives, the studies would have been impossible; however, without the inspired classroom practices, the recitation of theory would have been irrelevant. It is at the nexus of the two, combining theory with the study of classroom practice to produce theories of practice, where important teacher research happens. I would like to talk more about how this might look and what this might mean for classroom teachers interested in such a project.

Teacher Research, Action Research, Critical Research

Over the past 10 years, growing attention has been paid to teacher or practitioner research. Naturally, not all of this attention has been positive. Huberman (1996) exemplifies many of the recent critiques of practitioner research by questioning the ability of those who study their own practices to rise above their preconceptions and avoid distortions and self-delusion. It is not surprising that traditional researchers would take issue with the processes and political implications of practitioner research, for both call into question the legitimacy of traditional educational research. After all, if teachers take ownership over the enterprise of educational research, what does this mean for the future of university-based educators? Now, this does not have to be a zero-sum game; there is room for the practitioner-research traditions to exist in proximity to traditional educational research, but the concerns are logical and expected. What is surprising, however, is the amount of support practitioner-oriented research is receiving within the educational academy. Cochran-Smith and Lytle (1993), for instance, have asserted that teachers, as insiders, can offer special insights into the teaching and learning processes in schools that outside researchers are unable to provide. The acknowledgement, both positive and negative, are evidence that teacher-research matters and shows that teachers are becoming major players in the knowledge production process. This is indeed an exciting time to be involved in classroom-based research.

It is important to note that there is no one single tradition of practitioner research. Though they share some commonalities, there are multiple traditions of practitioner research. Zeichner and Noffke (2001) outline several of these traditions, such as action research, self-study, lesson study, and participatory research to name a few. In my experience, I have also participated in what is called critical research. In the following paragraphs, I only highlight two traditions, action research and critical research, but I encourage teachers to look into some of these other traditions to understand the many shapes that the revolution is taking.

Jean McNiff (1988) calls for an expansion of action research that encourages teachers to be reflective of practice in order to improve the quality of education for teachers and students. McNiff sees action research as a viable alternative to more traditional approaches to educational research. The traditional approach, she argues, reduces educational theory and research to separate disciplines of the sociology, psychology, history, and philosophy of education. Action research, on the other hand, approaches education as a unified exercise, seeing a teacher in class as the best judge of the total educational experience (p. 1).

Action research is part of a movement attempting to transform the onus of production of teacher knowledge to the teachers themselves. McNiff and other proponents of action research are unapologetic about veering from the traditional research paradigms that emerge from the social science and natural science paradigms. Generally, these disciplines acknowledge as researchers those who have certified credentials and use established methods to investigate the social and natural worlds. Given that teachers do not usually have this training and do not use the methods of social and natural science in the same ways that social and natural scientists do, their inquiry is often not accepted by participants in these disciplines as "rigorous" research. Therefore, it is more common for psychologists, sociologists, and anthropologists to have more ownership over teacher knowledge than the practitioners most closely associated with classroom practice.

McNiff (1988) argues that the social basis of action research is involvement and the educational basis is improvement. Its operation demands changes. Action research means action, both of the system under consideration and of the people involved in that system (p. 3). McNiff further argues that the validity of action research lies in the skills of the enquirer and is more personal and interpersonal than methodological (p.7). However, she rails against critics who claim that the approach is sloppy or soft. She responds to the challenges by claiming that action research has as its philosophical base an overarching awareness and respect for the integrity of individuals, a quality often lacking in more traditional approaches to educational research.

Although she acknowledges that action research cannot answer all of education's questions, many of which require traditional approaches, McNiff (1988) makes a strong argument for an action research tradition that can exist alongside more mainstream approaches to educational research. Indeed, action research can complement many traditional studies by offering unique perspectives and studies that are just not possible from any other vantage point than that of a classroom teacher. McNiff makes a distinction between theory-based approaches to educational research and action research that she advocates. While I respect the distinction, I do not see such a clear divide. However, I believe that teachers as action researchers use theories in different ways. Particularly, teachers as action researchers can draw upon many of the theoretical traditions of the social sciences that inform educational research. However, the purpose of the research is not to confirm or to disprove theories, but rather to use existing theories to develop *grounded theories* of exemplary educational practice. Strauss and Corbin (1988) define grounded theory as:

> [Theory where the] researcher begins with an area of study and allows the theory to emerge from the data. Theory derived from data is more likely to resemble the "reality" than is theory derived by putting together a series of concepts based on experience or solely through speculation (how one thinks things ought to work). Grounded theories, because they are drawn from data, are likely to offer insight, enhance understanding, and provide a meaningful guide to action.
> (p. 12)

In this respect, grounded theory offers a way to think about the social science disciplines and action research in a different light. Rather than see these disciplines at odds or action researchers on the margins of these traditions, Strauss and Corbin (1988) offer the perspective that the theories derived from action research can actually strengthen the disciplines. I would agree with them that, although the primary purpose of the research may be to improve the quality of education, action research also has much to offer to the disciplines of psychology, sociology, and anthropology.

Joe Kincheloe and Peter McLaren, in their chapter entitled "Rethinking Critical Theory and Qualitative Research" (1998) offer a brief introduction to critical theory while considering the possible implications for critical research. Critical research, they argue can best be understood in the context of the empowerment of individuals. Inquiry that aspires to the name "critical" must be connected to an attempt to confront the injustice of a particular society or sphere within the society. Research thus becomes a transformative endeavor unembarrassed by the label "political" and unafraid to consummate a relationship with an emancipatory consciousness (p. 264).

This is quite different from traditional research traditions that encourage objectivity and distance in the researcher. In fact, the critique most levied at practitioner-researchers is that teachers are too near the work of the classroom to be "objective" about its activities and participants. Critical research turns this argument on its head by arguing that only those who are close to a particular situation can truly understand it. According to the critical research tradition, teachers and students are most perfectly situated to conduct classroom research because they are the most interested and involved participants in classroom activity. As interested participants, they are also the most likely to promote research for social change, as opposed to research to inform the research community. It only makes sense that teachers and students conducting research want to improve classroom practice. The motives of traditional researchers, however, are not nearly so clear. Again, this is not to say that teachers should not allow traditional researchers into their classrooms. I am merely arguing for the legitimating of the critical research that involves teachers and students as political agents.

Critical researchers often regard their work as a first step toward forms of political action that can redress the injustices found in the field site or constructed in the very act of research itself. Thus critical researchers enter into an investigation with their assumptions on the table, so no one is confused concerning the epistemological and political baggage they bring with them to the research site. Critical research acknowledges the importance of the social location of the researcher to the nature of research. What I mean by this is that no researchers come to their site of research as blank slates, without opinions or values that influence what they look for and, indeed, what they find. I began this book by being upfront about my past relationship with popular culture as a youth. That was important for me to acknowledge because I was positively predisposed to the idea of incorporating popular culture into classrooms. Over time, I have remained positively predisposed. However, I have come to a greater understanding of the challenges involved in this project, and I have acquired a greater sensitivity to the multiple literacy demands placed on literate citizens in society and the need of classrooms to prepare students for these multiple demands.

Traditional researchers often influence research environments and outcomes in the very ways that they advocate against. There is usually not a mechanism in most traditional paradigms for theorizing the role of the researcher as a participant. Certainly the person in the back of the classroom with a notebook, the professor with the audio recorder asking questions, or the nature of the language on a survey influence outcomes, even when this is not intended by those conducting the research. A critical theorist would interject that, to the extent that researchers are unaware or unreflective of themselves as participants wielding power, their research stands the chance of reproducing existing power relations. Teachers, on the other hand, do not have the leisure to ignore their roles as power brokers in classroom research. Critical teacher research, then, does not have the illusion of a neutral activity that can be studied absent consideration of context and the participants. Indeed, much critical teacher research directly addresses the issues of power distribution and the role of teachers in this process.

Embracing critical postmodern goals of empowerment, Kincheloe and McLaren (1988) argue that workers can use critical research to uncover the way power operates to construct their everyday commonsense knowledge and to undermine their autonomy as professionals. Teachers as critical researchers can draw upon critical social theory to help them employ their understanding of their location in the institutional hierarchy in an effort to restructure the school as workplace. In this way, critical research is not only concerned with classroom curriculum and instruction, teachers can use critical research to question the very nature of schooling, including the disempowerment of teachers in many school settings. Together, teachers as critical researchers can work together to challenge, even to transform, these dehumanizing conditions when and where they exist. One of the core tenets of social theory is that it seeks to understand how people work together in transformative collective action. This collective does not always need to involve teachers and students in an isolated classroom. This collective action can take the form of teachers working together for change in their schools, in their profession, or even in society at large. Historically and internationally, teachers have played these types of roles vis-à-vis their societies and their students.

As critical researchers, teachers learn to teach themselves. In this context, learning in the workplace becomes a way of life, a part of the job. Not only is it important to share the learning from research with outside audiences, teachers can first share what they learn with local colleagues. The idea of teacher knowledge coming from within, though foreign to the workings of many schools, makes perfect sense within the critical tradition. As critical researchers, this does not mean that teachers turn away from outside knowledge, only that teachers are given an opportunity to learn from their own practice and to teach each other. Consider, for a moment, the implications for professional development if the experts came from within.

Finally, Kincheloe and McLaren (1988) discuss the importance of critical researchers having humility about themselves as researchers, about relationships between researchers and the subjects of research, and about the nature of critical inquiry. In light of this reflective humility, critical researchers do not search for some magic method of inquiry that will guarantee the validity of their findings. Traditional research, they contend, has focused on rigor to the neglect of the dynamics of the lived world—not to mention the pursuit of justice in the lived world. Trustworthiness, many have argued, is a more appropriate word to use in the context of critical research. It is helpful because it signifies a different set of assumptions about research purposes than a focus on objective validity might indicate.

Trustworthiness, as it is used here, can have multiple meanings, each of them important. One meaning of trustworthiness could entail the relationship between the researcher and the subjects of research. Although in traditional research, trustworthiness normally refers to the data, a critical researcher may be concerned with the levels of trust in the personal relationships developed during the research process. A second meaning of trustworthiness, directly related to the first, concerns the amount of trust a critical researcher can have in the conclusions that she or he has drawn from a particular set of data. This level of confidence can certainly be increased to the degree that the researcher has confidence in the relationships that have been established and the nature of involvement. A teacher, for instance, who has developed intimate relationships with students over an extended period can have more confidence in her conclusions than, say, a researcher who visits once every other week who has not developed either trust or relationships with the classroom participants.

As you can see, there are many similarities among these parallel research traditions. Each challenges, to some degree, preconceived notions of who has the right to conduct "legitimate" research and what this legitimate, rigorous research looks like. They also all argue for the importance of teacher-researchers to knowledge production and the improvement of educational practice. Further, each is situated in action and sees research as valuable only to the extent that it involves action and commitment to educational change. They differ somewhat in their philosophical antecedents and the explicit relationships to politics and social change. Whichever tradition you acknowledge, however, the call to action is the same.

A Call to Action

The call to action for teachers to become practitioner-researchers is itself an activist stance; however, teachers will need to become activists merely to acquire the tools and space necessary to become involved in the traditions of research advocated here. Part of being an activist entails demanding more resources for on-site research and professional development. Great teachers are good at demanding resources for their students, and this is obviously important. It is also important, however, that they begin to demand resources for themselves. For instance, most secondary schools have libraries for students, but very few have ample libraries for teachers. In order to engage in the kind of work that I am advocating, teachers need access to educational journals, trade books, and academic texts that offer important background information and exemplary models of teacher research. The proximity of available research, I argue, would greatly increase the consumption and production of teacher-initiated literacy research, which would be beneficial for teachers, for schools, for the discipline, and, most importantly, for the students who will benefit from improved practice. For a nominal fee, a secondary school can obtain institutional memberships to a handful of organizations (such as the National Council of Teachers of English, the International Reading Association, the National Reading Conference, the Council on Educational Anthropology, and the American Educational Research Association) that would then allow teachers access to the most recent educational research. A small annual budget would allow for the purchases of important books. Most secondary schools receive annual catalogs from major publishers of research on adolescent literacy. If not, it is fairly simple to either call or go online to request catalogs.

Also, with the onset of the cyberspace revolution, more resources are being made available online. For example, the National Council of Teachers of English offers Co-LEARN (**C**enters **o**f **L**iteracy **E**ducation **A**chievement, **R**esearch, and **N**etworking), an online professional development program available to teachers if their institutions sign up for it. Of course, teachers will need computers and high-speed internet access in order to adequately participate in these virtual communities. At some point, however, we, as citizens, must demand that society invest more in teachers as professionals, ensuring that they have the tools that they need to be successful practitioners. I am arguing that part of what teachers need are the tools to consume and produce practitioner-initiated, classroom-based research.

As researchers and textual producers, teachers can present their work at department meetings or regional and national conferences; they can write articles for publication in practitioner journals or books such as this one that address the world of possibilities for powerful and transformational practice in America's literacy classrooms. Teachers, as researchers, can present to the world classrooms in which diversity and the messiness of life are generative substance rather than obstacles to be overcome. Where the everyday, the social, and the cultural are not add-ons, but central to the curriculum and students can acquire valuable skills for citizenship, academic advancement, professional membership, and artistic expression as they encounter a complement of classical, contemporary, and popular texts.

I recognize that this is asking a great deal from teachers, but no one said that this was going to be easy. I have, throughout this book, deliberated to make the case, not for the simple, but for the possible. And I conclude, not with parting wisdom, but with a call to action for you, the readers, the teachers of today and tomorrow, to draw upon theory, research, and practical experience to articulate a vision of twenty-first century literacy classrooms that use, among others, the critical teaching of popular culture to help tomorrow's citizens exist more powerfully in the world. Most importantly, I offer to you, in the midst of dismal and dark forecasts for America's educational future, plausible rays of hope.

References

Adorno, T. (1991). *The culture industry*. London: Routledge.

Adorno, T., & Horkheimer, M. (1999). The culture industry: Enlightenment as mass deception. In S. During (Ed.), *The cultural studies reader*. New York: Routledge, 31–41.

Alvermann, D. (2001). *Effective literacy instruction for adolescents*. Executive Summary and Paper Commissioned by the National Reading Conference. Chicago: National Reading Conference.

Apple, M. (1990). *Ideology and curriculum, 2nd ed*. New York: Routledge.

Apple, M. (1996). *Cultural politics and education*. New York: Teachers College Press.

Appleman, D. (2000). *Critical encounters in high school English: Teaching literary theory to adolescents*. New York: Teachers College Press.

Aristotle (1991). *The art of rhetoric*. New York: Penguin.

Aronowitz, S., & Giroux, H. (1991). *Postmodern education*. Minneapolis: University of Minnesota Press.

Atkinson, J. W. (1957). Motivational determinants of risk-taking behavior. *Psychological Review, 64*, 359–372.

Atkinson, J. W. (1964). *An introduction to motivation*. Princeton, NJ: Van Nostrand.

Baker, H. A. (1993). *Black studies, rap, and the academy*. Chicago: University of Chicago Press.

Bandura, A. (1986). *Social foundations of thought and action: A social cognitive theory*. Englewood Cliffs, NJ: Prentice Hall.

Bandura, A. (1997). *Self-efficacy: The exercise of control*. New York: Freeman.

Barton, D. (2000). Researching literacy practices: Learning from activities with teachers and students. In D. Barton, M. Hamilton, & R. Ivanic (Eds.), *Situated literacies: Reading and writing in context* New York: Routledge, 167–179.

Barton, D., & Hamilton, M. (1998). *Local literacies: Reading and writing in one community*. New York: Routledge.

Barton, D., & Hamilton, M. (2000). Literacy practices. (pp. 7–15). In D. Barton, M. Hamilton, & R. Ivanic (Eds.), *Situated literacies: Reading and writing in context*, New York: Routledge.

Berg, B. L. (2001). *Qualitative research methods for the social sciences*. Boston: Allyn & Bacon.

Best, S., & Kellner, D. (1991). *Postmodern theory: Critical interrogations*. New York: Guilford.

Biklen, S. K. & Bogdan, R. C. (1998). *Qualitative research in education.* Needham Heights, MA: Allyn & Bacon.

Bourdieu, P., & Wacquant, L. J. D. (1992). *An invitation to reflexive sociology.* Chicago, IL: University of Chicago Press.

Campbell, R. (2002). *Media and culture: An introduction to mass communication.* Boston: Bedford-St. Martins.

Carspecken, P. F. (1996). *Critical ethnography in educational research: A theoretical and practical guide.* New York: Routledge.

Casey, B., Casey, N., Calvert, B., French, L., & Lewis, J. (2002). *Television studies: Key concepts.* London: Routledge.

Cochran-Smith, M., & Lytle, S. (1993). *Inside outside: Teacher research and knowledge.* New York: Teachers College Press.

Cohen, D., & Neufield, B. (1981). The failure of high schools and the progress of education. *Dedalus, 110,* 61–90.

Cole, M. (1996). *Cultural psychology: A once and future discipline.* Cambridge, MA: Harvard University Press.

Coppola, F. F. (1972). The *godfather* [film]. Los Angeles: Paramount Pictures.

Coppola, F. F. (1974). The *godfather part II* [film]. Los Angeles: Paramount Pictures.

Coppola, F. F. (1990). The *godfather part III* [film]. Los Angeles: Paramount Pictures.

Corey, M., & Ochoa, G. (2002). *The American film institute desk reference.* New York: DK Publishers.

Cushman, E., Kingten, E., Kroll, B., & Rose, M. (2001). Introduction: Surveying the field. In E. Cushman, E. Kingten, B. Kroll, & M. Rose (Eds.), *Literacy: A critical sourcebook.* Boston: Bedford/St. Martins.

Darling-Hammond, L. (1998). New standards, old inequalities: The current challenge for African-American education. *The state of Black America report.* Chicago: National Urban League.

Darling-Hammond, L. (2000). *Solving the dilemmas of teacher supply, demand, and standards: How we can ensure a competent, caring, and qualified teacher for every child.* New York: National Commission on Teaching and America's Future.

Darder, A. (1991). *Culture and power in the classroom: A critical foundation for bicultural education.* Westport, CT: Bergin and Garvey.

Delpit, L. (1988). The silenced dialogue: Power and pedagogy in educating other people's children. *Harvard Educational Review, 58,* 3, 280–298.

Delpit, L. (1995). *Other people's children: Cultural conflict in the classroom.* New York: The New Press.

Dewey, J. (1956). *The school and society.* Chicago: University of Chicago Press.

Docker, J. (1994). *Postmodernism and popular culture: A cultural history.* New York: Cambridge University Press.

During, S. (1999). Introduction. (pp. 1–30) In S. During (Ed.), *The cultural studies reader*. New York: Routledge,.

Eccles, J. (1983). Expectancies, values and academic behaviors. In J. T. Spence (Ed.), *Achievement and achievement motives*. San Francisco: Freeman, 75–146

Eccles, J., Wigfield, A., Flanagan, C., Miller, C., Reuman, D., & Yee, D. (1989). Self-concepts, domain values, and self-esteem: Relations and change at early adolescence. *Journal of Personality, 57*, 283–310.

Farley, C. (1999). Hip-hop nation: There's more to rap than just rhythms and rhymes. After two decades, it has transformed the culture of America. *Time, 153* (5), 55–65.

Ferdman, B.M. (1990). Literacy and cultural identity. *Harvard Educational Review, 60* (2), 181–204.

Freire, P. (1970). *Pedagogy of the oppressed*. New York: Continuum.

Freire, P. (1997). *Teachers as cultural workers: Letters to those who dare teach*. Boulder, CO: Westview.

Freire, P., & Macedo, D. (1987). *Reading the word and the world*. Westport, CT: Bergin & Garvey.

Foster, M. (1998). *Black teachers on teaching*. New York: New Press.

Gee, J. (1996). *Social linguistics and literacies: Ideology in discourses*. London: Routledge Falmer.

Geertz, C. (2000). *Local knowledge: Further essays in interpretive anthropology*. New York: Basic Books.

George, N. (1999). *Hiphopamerica*. New York: Penguin Putnam.

Giroux, H. A. (1988). *Teachers as intellectuals: Toward a critical pedagogy of learning*. New York: Bergin and Garvey.

Giroux, H. A. (1996). *Fugitive cultures: Race, violence, and youth*. New York: Routledge.

Giroux, H. A. (1997). Border pedagogy and the age of postmodernism. *Pedagogy and the politics of hope*. Boulder, CO: Westview, 147–163.

Gramsci, A. (1971). *Selections from prison notebooks*. London: New Left Books.

Gumperz, J., & Hymes, D. (Eds.) (1986). *Directions in sociolinguistics: The ethnography of communication*. New York: Blackwell.

Hall, S. (1998). Notes on deconstructing the popular. In J. Storey (Ed.), *Cultural theory and popular culture: A reader*. Athens: University of Georgia Press, 442–453.

Harris, T., & Hodges, R. (Eds.). (1995). *The literacy dictionary: The vocabulary of reading and writing*. Newark, DE: International Reading Association.

Heath, S. B. (1983) *Ways with words: Language, life, and work in communities and classrooms*. Cambridge: Cambridge University Press.

Hilliard, A. (2003). No mystery: Closing the achievement gap between Africans and excellence. In T. Perry, C. Steele, & A. Hilliard (Eds.), *Young, gifted, and black: Promoting high achievement among African-American students*. Boston: Beacon, 131–165.

Hodder, I. (1998). The interpretation of documents and material culture. In N. Denzin & Y. Lincoln (Eds.), *Collecting and interpreting qualitative materials*. Thousand Oaks, CA: Sage Publications, 110–129.

hooks, b. (1994). *Teaching to transgress: Education as the practice of freedom*. New York: Routledge.

Horkheimer, M. (1972). Traditional and critical theory. *Critical theory: Selected essays*. New York: Seabury Press.

Huberman, M. (1996). Moving mainstream: Taking a closer look at teacher research. *Language Arts, 73*, 124–140.

Hudson, M. & Holmes, B. (1994). Missing teachers, impaired communities: The unanticipated consequences of Brown vs. board of education on the African American teaching force at the precollegiate level. *Journal of Negro Education, 63* (3), 388–393.

Hull, G. (1993). Critical literacy and beyond: Lessons learned from students and workers in a vocational program and on the job. *Anthropology and Education Quarterly, 24* (4), 308–317.

Hunter-Boykin, H. (1992). Responses to the African American teacher shortage: 'We grow our own' through the teacher preparation program at Coolidge High School. *Journal of Negro Education, 61* (4), 483–493.

Hymes, D. (1999) (Ed.). *Reinventing anthropology*. Ann Arbor: University of Michigan Press.

Jameson, F. (1999). Nostalgia for the Present. In J. Wolfreys (Ed.), *Literary theories: A reader and guide*. New York: NYU Press, 395–409.

Kellner, D. (1995). *Media culture: Cultural studies, identity and politics between the modern and the postmodern*. New York: Routledge.

Kellner, D., & Durham, M. (2001). Adventures in media and cultural studies: Introducing the keyworks. In M. Durham & D. Kellner (Eds.), *Media and cultural studies keyworks*. Oxford: Blackwell, 1–31.

Kincheloe, J. L., & McLaren, P. (1998). Rethinking critical qualitative research. In N. Denzin & Y. Lincoln (Eds.), *The landscape of qualitative research: Theories and issues*. Thousand Oaks, CA: Sage, 260–299.

Ladson-Billings, G. (1994*). The dreamkeepers: Successful teachers of African American children*. San Francisco: Jossey-Bass.

Lave, J., & Wenger, E. (1991). *Situated learning: Legitimate peripheral participation*. Cambridge: Cambridge University Press.

LeCompte, M., & Schensul, J. (1999). *Designing and conducting ethnographic research*. Walnut Creek, CA: Altamira Press.

Lee, C. (1992*). Signifying as a scaffold for literary interpretation: The pedagogical implications of an African American discourse genre*. Urbana, IL: NCTE Press.

Lee, C. & Smagorinsky, P. (2000). Introduction. In C. Lee & P. Smagorinsky (Eds.), *Vygotskian perspectives on literacy research: Constructing meaning through collaborative inquiry*. New York: Cambridge University Press, 1–18.

Light, A. (Ed.) (1999). *The Vibe history of hip-hop*. New York: Three Rivers Press.

Lipsitz, G. (1994). History, hip-hop, and the post-colonial politics of sound. *Dangerous crossroads: Popular music, postmodernism, and the poetics of place.* New York: Verso, 23–48.

Mahiri, J. (1998). *Shooting for excellence: African American and youth culture in new century schools.* New York: Teachers College Press.

Marx, K. (1973). *Grundrisse: Foundations of the critique of political economy.* New York: Penguin.

McCarthy, C. (1998). *The uses of culture: Education and the limits of ethnic affiliation.* New York: Routledge.

McCaughey, M., & Ayers, M. (2003). *Cyberactivism: Online activism in theory and practice.* New York: Routledge.

McLaren, P. (1994). *Life in schools: An introduction to critical pedagogy in the foundations of education.* New York: Longman.

McNeil, L. M. (2000). *Contradictions of school reform: Educational costs of standardized testing.* New York: Routledge.

McNiff, J. (1988). *Action research: Principles and practices.* London: Routledge.

Meikle, G. (2002). *Future active: Media activism and the internet.* London: Routledge.

Merriam, S. B. (1998). *Qualitative research and case study applications in education.* San Francisco: Jossey-Bass.

Moll, L. (2000). Inspired by Vygotsky: Ethnographic experiments in education. In C. Lee & P. Smagorinsky (Eds.), *Vygotskian perspectives on literacy research: Constructing meaning through collaborative inquiry.* New York: Cambridge University Press, 256–268.

Morrell, E. (2002). Toward a critical pedagogy of popular culture: Implications for academic and critical literacy development among urban youth. *Journal of Adolescent and Adult Literacy, 46* (1), 72–77.

Morrell, E. (2003). Legitimate peripheral participation as professional development: Lessons from a summer research seminar. *Teacher Education Quarterly 30* (2), 89–99.

Morrell, E., & Duncan-Andrade, J. (2002). Toward a critical classroom discourse: Promoting academic literacy through engaging hip-hop culture with urban youth. *English Journal, 91* (6), 88–94.

Morrison, T. (1993). *Playing in the dark: Whiteness and the literary imagination.* New York: Vintage.

Nas. (1996). *It Was Written.* New York: Columbia Records.

National Center for Education Statistics (1998a). *Digest of education statistics.* Washington, DC.

National Center for Education Statistics. (1998b). *Projection of education statistics to 2008.* Washington, DC.

National Council of Teachers of English/International Reading Association. (1996). *Standards for the English language arts.* Urbana, IL: NCTE.

New London Group. (1996). A pedagogy of multiliteracies: Designing social futures. *Harvard Educational Review, 66* (1), 60–92.

Nieto, S. (1996). *Affirming diversity: The sociopolitical context of multicultural education, 2nd ed.* White Plains, NY: Longman.

Oakes, J., & Lipton, M. (1999). *Teaching to change the world.* Boston: McGraw-Hill.

Orenstein, P. (1995). *Schoolgirls.* New York: Anchor Books.

Pattison, R. (1982). *On literacy: The politics of the word from Homer to the age of rock.* New York: Oxford University Press.

Pintrich, P., & Schunk, D. (2002). *Motivation in education: Theory, research, and applications.* Upper Saddle River, NJ: Merrill/Prentice Hall.

Powell, C. T. (1991). Rap Music: An Education with a beat from the street. *Journal of Negro Education, 60* (3), 245–259.

Rogoff, B. (1990). *Apprenticeship in thinking: Cognitive development in social context.* Oxford: Oxford University Press.

Rose, T. (1991). Fear of a Black Planet: Rap music and Black cultural politics in the 1990s. *Journal of Negro Education, 60* (3), 277–291.

Rose, T. (1994). *Black noise: Rap music and Black culture in contemporary America.* Hanover, NH: University Press of New England.

Sardar, Z., & Van Loon, B. (2000). *Introducing media studies.* New York: Totem.

Scholes, R. (1998). *The rise and fall of English: Reconstructing English as a discipline.* New Haven, CT: Yale University Press.

Shor, I. (1992). *Empowering education: Critical teaching for social change.* Chicago: University of Chicago Press.

Smith, K., & Stock, P. (2003). Trends and issues in research in the teaching of the English language arts. In J. Flood, D. Lapp, J. Squire, & J. Jensen (Eds.), *Handbook of research on teaching the English language arts, 2nd ed.* Mahwah, NJ: Lawrence Earlbaum Associates, 114–130.

Steele, C. (2003). Stereotype threat and African-American student achievement. In T. Perry, C. Steele, & A. Hilliard (Eds.), *Young, gifted, and black: Promoting high achievement among African-American students.* Boston: Beacon, 109–130.

Sterling, B. (1992). *The hacker crackdown: Law and disorder on the electronic frontier.* New York: Bantam.

Storey, J. (1998). *An introduction to cultural theory and popular culture.* Athens: University of Georgia Press.

Strauss, A., & Corbin, J. (1998). *Basics of qualitative research: Techniques and procedures for developing grounded theory.* Thousand Oaks, CA: Sage Publications.

Street, B. V. (1995). *Literacy in theory and practice.* Cambridge: Cambridge University Press.

The Refugee Camp. (1996). *The Score* [Compact Disc]. New York: Columbia Records.

Tyack, D., & Cuban, L. (1995). *Tinkering toward utopia: A century of public school reform.* Cambridge, MA: Harvard University Press.

UNESCO (1975). *Final report for international symposium for literacy.* Persepolis, Iran.

Venezky, R. L., Wagner, D. A., & Ciliberti, B. S. (Eds.). (1990*). Toward defining literacy.* Newark, DE: International Reading Association.

Vygotsky, L. (1978). *Mind in society.* Cambridge, MA: Harvard University Press.

Wenger, E. (1998). *Communities of practice: Learning, meaning and identity.* Cambridge: Cambridge University Press.

Wigfield, A. (1994). Expectancy-value theory of achievement motivation: A developmental perspective. *Educational Psychology Review, 6,* 49–78.

Wigfield, A., & Eccles, J. (1992). The development of achievement task values: A theoretical analysis. *Developmental Review, 12,* 265–310.

Wigfield, A., & Eccles, J. (2000). Expectancy-value theory of achievement motivation. *Contemporary Educational Psychology, 25,* 68–81.

Wilhelm. G. (1997) *You gotta be the book: Teaching engaged and reflective reading with adolescents.* New York: Teachers College Press.

Williams, B. (2002). *Tuned in: Television and the teaching of writing.* Portsmouth, NH: Boynton/Cook Heinemann.

Williams, R. (1995). *The sociology of culture.* Chicago: University of Chicago Press.

Williams, R. (1998). The analysis of culture. In J. Storey (Ed.), *Cultural theory and popular culture: A reader.* Athens: University of Georgia Press, 48–56.

Zeichner, K., & Noffke, S. (2001). Practitioner research. In V. Richardson (Ed.), *Handbook of research on teaching, 4th ed.* Washington, DC: American Educational Research Association, 298–352.

Appendix A

Poet in Society Unit Plans and Assignments

Rationale

Educational Research Indicates:

1. Students are more inclined to be motivated to participate in activities they perceive as immediately relevant and personal;
2. Hip-hop music is a genre of music worthy of academic contemplation and study; and
3. Hip-hop music enjoys tremendous popularity among today's youth for its entertainment value and pertinent themes.

This unit has been designed to incorporate hip-hop music and poetry into a "traditional" senior English poetry unit in order to:

1. Increase motivation and participation in discussions and assignments;
2. Teach critical essay writing and literary terminology in the context of hip-hop music and canonical poetry;
3. Situate hip-hop music and culture historically and socially and discuss its inception as youth's response to urban post-industrialism;
4. Encourage youth to view elements of popular culture through a critical lens and to help these students to critique messages sent to them through the popular media; and
5. Help students to understand the intellectual integrity, literary merit, and social commentary contained within their own popular culture.

Goals and Objectives

- To cover the poetry of the Elizabethan Age, the Puritan Revolution, and the Romantics, which are part of the district-mandated curriculum for 12th-grade English, and which students will be expected to have a knowledge of on the Advanced Placement Exam and in college English courses;

- To gain a greater understanding of canonical poets in the context of the literary and historical periods in which they wrote;

- To discuss and gain a greater awareness of the role poets and their poetry play in providing social commentary;

- To use the ideas and language of poetry and song as a vehicle to expository writing;

- To develop skills associated with oral and written arguments, the ability to work efficiently in groups, and the ability to deliver formal presentations;

- To teach students how to critique poems and songs in a critical essay;

- To help students develop note-taking skills in lectures and presentations; and

- To help students develop confidence in composing in a variety of poetic forms.

Major Student Activities

- **Group Poetry Presentations**—Students are divided into groups of 5–6 and given one week to analyze a poem and hip-hop text and create a presentation for their classmates. Students are asked to compare and contrast the poem and hip-hop texts in terms of content, themes, and structure. At the culmination of their week's preparation, students are then asked to present for 30 minutes and to facilitate a conversation with their classmates for the final 20 minutes of a class period.

- **Presentation Notes and Evaluations**—Students are required to take notes on all of the presentations (except their own) and submit a descriptive evaluation of these presentations. As part of their group assignment, they are asked to generate potential questions for each of the other groups. This helps to promote substantive conversation after the presentations. It also helps non-presenters to pay attention while developing an important college-readiness skill. Finally, it is a way to reward students for meaningful classroom participation.

- **5–7 Page Critical Essay on a Song of Students' Choice**—Students must submit transcribed song lyrics along with their essay.
- **Anthology of 10 Original Poems Including:**
  1. An Elegy
  2. A Ballad
  3. A Sonnet
  4. A Poem That Describes a Familiar Place
  5. A Poem That Conveys a Mood
  6. A Poem That deals With a Political, Social, or Economic Problem
  7. A Love Poem
  8. A Poem that Celebrates a Particular Facet of Life
  9. Open Poem
  10. Open Poem
- **Oral Poetry Reading** Each student selects five of the poems contained in their anthology to present to the class in an oral reading. Students are asked to briefly introduce each poem, explaining its genre and inspiration.

Minor Activities

- **Metaphors** —Students work in pairs to create 25 metaphors to complete the statement, "Love is . . ." Groups present their work as a way to talk about the importance of metaphor to writing poetry.
- **Similes**—Students work in small groups to develop similes to complete the statement, "When you left me, I felt like . . ." Students are challenged to write similes that are at least five words. Students share their work as a way to talk about the use of similes in poetry.
- **Conveying an Emotion**—Students, in small groups, are given an emotion (i.e., love, hate, fear, paranoia, depression, excitement, grief, patient endurance) about which they are to construct a poem. The catch is that the students cannot use the

particular word in their poem. During the latter half of the activity, groups read their poems to the class, which is supposed to guess the emotion. Each group also explains the choices they made in the creation of the poem.

- **Vivid Imagery**—Students are to choose a scene and then create 10 vivid images to convey that scene. Again, students are asked not to use the words that name the scene in their work. Students share their poems with classmates who attempt to guess the scene and also talk about the construction, appropriateness, and effectiveness of the images.

Appendix B

Race and Justice Unit Plans and Assignments

Casebooks (To be handed in at the culmination of the trial) should include:

- An opening statement
- At least three questions you would ask of each of your witnesses and your witnesses response to these questions
- At least three questions you anticipate the opposing side asking your witnesses in a cross-examination
- At least three questions you plan to ask the opposing witnesses in your own cross-examination
- Copious (thorough) Trial Notes
- A 3–5-page closing statement/ analysis of the court trial

Grades for the trial are as follows:
100 points—Trial participation
150 points—Casebook

Appendix C

Odyssey/Godfather Final Examination

Part I–50 points

Pick 10 of the following characters from *The Odyssey* and *The Godfather* to identify. Explain who they are, what they do, and how they are significant to the epic. At least five IDs must be from each work (5 pts. each).

Antinous	Mentor
Calypso	Mosca
Cardinal Lumberto	Nausicaa
Connie (Corleone)	Orestes
Don Lucchesi	Polyphemus
Eumaeus	Poseidon
Grace Hamilton	Vincent Mancini
Mary Corleone	

Part II–100 points

Pick one of the following sides to argue making specific references to the text and film when appropriate (50 points).

1. *The Odyssey* and *The Godfather* are classic epic tales where Odysseus and Michael Corleone are characterized as epic heroes.

   Or

2. *The Odyssey* and *The Godfather*, although classic epics, provide ample critiques of Odysseus and Michael Corleone as epic heroes.

Make the following argument using specific textual and film references (50 points).

Although females during the periods when *The Odyssey* and *The Godfather* were written were subordinated to the men, the major females (and goddesses) in these two epics are able to manipulate the power dynamics to achieve the results they desired.

Appendix D

North Bay Fall Semester
Study Sheet and Final Examination

FINAL EXAM REVIEW, FALL SEMESTER, ENGLISH IV-P

A. Identifications (5 points each) 1. Who or where? 2. What is the function? 3. Why is it significant? To receive full credit for the IDs, you must be able to identify the role that the character/place plays in its respective work and the significance of that character or place to the larger themes and issues discussed in the work.

Stand and Deliver: Jaime Escalante, Angel, Finger Man, Johnny Frank, Anita Delgado, Mayo, Sra. Molina, Mr. Suzaki, P.E./Math teacher, The Principal, Mr. Delgado, Claudia; Sophia, Jaime's neighbor, Claudia's mom, Sophia's mom.

Savage Inequalities: Jonathan Kozol

Canterbury Tales: Chaucer, Knight, Squire, Yeoman, Monk, Friar, Prioress, Miller, Parson, Wife of Bath, Canterbury, Henry II, Thomas Beckett, Pilgrimage, Franklin.

Othello: Shakespeare, Othello, Desdemona, Iago, Roderigo, Cassio, Brabantio, Montano, Emilia, Bianca, Duke, Lodovico.

The Godfather: Don Vito Corleone, Mama Corleone, Sonny, Fredo, Michael Corleone, Connie Corleone, Tom Hagen, Kay Adams, Viril Sollozzo, Jack Woltz, McClusky, Luca Brasi, Johnny Fontaine, Carlo Rizzi, Appolonia, Don Tommasino, Peter Clemenza, Tessio, Don Barzini, Bruno Tattaglia, Coppola, Viteli, Bonasera, Bridesmaid, Enzo, the baker.

B. Be thoroughly familiar with the plot, setting, authors, major and minor characters, literary terms, and literary periods of each work. Also, explain how the elements of cinematography (i.e., camera angles, light vs. dark imagery, music selection, foreground/background, and so on) lend to the interpretations of the films.

C. Be able to identify key quotes and passages from both the films and literary works. To receive full credit, you will need to name the speaker, the context, and the significance of the quote/passage to the work and to the themes/issues discussed in class this semester.

D. Have a knowledge and understanding of the major conflicts and issues involved in each work. Also, you must be able to show how a given conflict or issue evolves or functions in a stated work and compare/contrast how certain conflicts or issues evolve in a number of works (i.e., Role/Treatment of Women, Characterization of America and American values).

E. Compare and contrast protagonists/antagonists, themes, and issues from one work to another. Look at overarching and repetitive themes.

FINAL EXAMINATION, ENGLISH IV-P
(Untracked English Class), 250 pts.

Identifications–100 pts. (5pts. Each)

1. Angel	2. Sra. Molina	3. Jaime Escalante	4. Thomas Beckett
5. Knight	6. Wife of Bath	7. Don Barzini	8. Tom Hagen
9. Roderigo	10. Kozol	11. Brabantio	12. Appolonia
13. Yeoman	14. Iago	15. Bianca	16. Chaucer
17. Emilia	18. Montano	19. Virgil Solozza	20. Luca Brasi

Essay Section

1. Analyze the following quotation, giving its speaker, context, and greater significance to the overall work and themes and issues discussed in class this semester:

    a. "Do you spend time with your family? Because a man who doesn't spend time with his family can never be a real man." (20 points)

    b. "East St. Louis is, according to a teacher at the University of Southern Illinois, 'a repository for a nonwhite population that is now regarded as expendable.' The Post Dispatch describes it as 'America's Soweto.'" (20 points)

2. In a brief essay response, compare/contrast the characters Othello and Don Vito Corleone as tragic heroes. How does each live up to this distinction? In what ways are they similar as tragic heroes? In what crucial ways are they different? (35 points)

3. The subjugation or marginalization of the female is a recurring theme of many of the novels, films, plays, and essays.

Using three works covered in class this year, select female characters that are subjugated and marginalized in their society. In a critical essay, analyze these characters and the roles they play in their respective works. How specifically are they marginalized or subjugated? What similarities do they have as characters? How are they different? How do each character's experiences reinforce the idea of male domination? In what ways do these characters resist this domination? Do not summarize the plot or action of the work you choose. (75 points)

Appendix E

North Bay High Syllabus (Regular, Untracked Class)

Senior English—A Course Outline
1997–1998

Instructor: Mr. Morrell
School Phone: 000-0000
Home Phone: (000) 000-0000

Course Text

Elements of Literature—Sixth Course, Literature of Britain
The core of the class will be British Literature and Contemporary American Literature.

Recommended Materials

1. Standard dictionary and thesaurus
2. Binder paper
3. A three-ring binder or folder to keep all written assignments
4. Notebook

Themes, Procedures, Major Activities/Goals

- Exploring cultural and personal identity through literature, film, expository, and fictional writing
- Learning to more effectively express one's self through the written and spoken medium
- College Preparation—The (P) in English IV-P (HP) stands for college prep, so the class will be run accordingly, including:
  1. College Entrance Essays
  2. SAT/ ACT Preparation
  3. College Prep Vocabulary
  4. Essay examinations
- Introduction to literary criticism and interpretation as well as literary terminology

- Literature as it pertains to life: How are the ideas/themes/ issues discussed in this literary work relevant to 17 and 18 year olds in North Bay City, CA, in 1997–1998?
- Engage in discussion and debate over issues brought up in literature, film, and society
- Panels/Oral Presentations
- Senior Project—will consist of a major portfolio project to be completed during the second semester
- Resume Workshop
- Book Analyses—one completed by the fifth week of each marking period
- Advance Placement Exam Preparation—the AP exam is open to anyone who wants to take it and offers 6 semester units of college credit to all who pass (a $4,000 value!). We will spend time preparing for this exam and you should feel ready to take it in May should you choose to do so

Planned Units
Summer 1997
- Summer reading includes *Song of Solomon* and *Savage Inequalities*
- Summer writing includes draft of College Entrance Essay

Fall 1997
- *Savage Inequalities* (in America's Educational System) and *Stand and Deliver*
- *Canterbury Tales* a Medieval epic and *Dances With Wolves*
- *The Odyssey* by Homer and *The Godfather* Trilogy
- *Othello* by William Shakespeare

Spring 1998
- *A Time To Kill* the movie and *Native Son* by Richard Wright
- Poet in Society Unit (Includes hip-hop music and culture)
- *The Big Aieeee/The Kitchen God's Wife* by Amy Tan
- *Apocalypse Now* the movie and *Heart of Darkness* by Joseph Conrad
- Final Portfolio Project

Grading

Every assignment will have a point value. At the end of the grading period when the points are totaled, 90% = A, 80% = B, and so on.

Late Work

Unless accompanied by an excused absence, work will be docked 10% (one grade) for each day it is late, up to 50%. After one week, assignments will no longer be accepted.

Attendance and Class Rules

In addition to the school rules which all apply, the class rules simply are to:
1. Respect others
2. Respect yourself

If you respect others, you will allow them access to the wealth of knowledge available in the class and a forum that is safe to express ideas freely and openly without fear. If you respect yourself, you will take advantage of the same opportunities. Willful disrespect for anyone (teachers, students, guests, etc.) at any time will not be tolerated!

Continuous tardiness and unexcused absences will affect both your citizenship and scholarship grades. Seven unexcused absences in any marking period will result in failure (a scholarship grade of F) for that marking period. You have five (5) days after returning from an absence to clear it.

Publishing

North Bay High has its own literary magazine that publishes outstanding student work. Also, there will be various contests occurring throughout the year and I will be alerting interested students. Hopefully, we will have a great deal published from our classes.

In Closing

This promises to be an exciting year for you for many reasons. Hopefully, this class will add to that excitement. Ultimately, though, the class will be what you students make of it.

Appendix F

Guidelines for Summer Seminar Final Presentations
(Used for Hip-Hop Project and Media Project)

Introduction

- **The Problem (Justification for the Research)**—This should be the initial portion of the introduction where you explain the relevance of the research you are conducting.
- **The Research Question**—Given the need for the research, what specific question is your study attempting to answer? Why is your question significant or important?

Literature Review

Upon what theories or prior studies are you basing your research? What are the terms or concepts that need defining? How does your study build on these theories and concepts?

Methods

Describe in detail, the schools, classrooms, students, politicians, activists, community members, and other entities that you encountered in your study. To ensure anonymity, choose pseudonyms for the schools and all people you include in the study.

Explain the process or method your paper will employ to explore the question that you have asked? Will you conduct interviews, surveys, perform ethnographic research, or design an experiment? What is the rationale behind your methodology?

Reporting of Findings

This is the body or meat of your paper where you introduce, cite, synthesize, and critique the data that you collect.

Conclusion

What significance do these findings hold for educational policy and research? What do these findings suggest about the broader issue of youth access? What further research would you suggest? How would you like to pursue these issues in the 2000–2001 school year?

Based on your expert status, you need to take some leadership and exert some authority to help solve the problems you mention in your introduction.

References

- You are required to have a minimum of three (3) references to readings.
- All papers will use the APA style.

Appendix G

Media Survey–Summer Seminar 2000

(Created and distributed by students at the Democratic National Convention)

To Whom It May Concern:

I am a West Coast University Research Fellow in a college summer enrichment program examining various perspectives about youth, youth issues, and youth protesters in the media. If you could please take a few minutes to answer 10 questions it would be greatly appreciated.

Date:_____ Time:_____ Location/Site:_____

Age: __ 10-14 __ 15-20 __ 21-29 __ 30-39 __ Over 40
Role: __ student __ protester __ delegate __ media __ resident
__ official __ police __ employee __bystander __ other

For Media Personnel:

Specific Role:_____

Employer: _____

1. Recalling a recent story involving youth (10–21 years old), youth issues, and/or youth protesters, what was the main topic/focus of the story?

_____
_____
_____

2. What did you learn about youth in the story?

_____
_____
_____

3. How did the story talk about youth in relation to the particular issue?

_____

_____

_____

4. Please list all who were called upon as "experts" in the story.

_____

_____

_____

5. What others were called upon as informants in the story?

_____

_____

_____

6. Can the media's/author's/reporter's positionality (i.e., race, class, gender, community of residence, or employment) affect how the youth are presented in stories? (Circle one)

Always   Sometimes   Very Seldom   Never

7. Who are the primary subjects of the recent stories featuring youth?

_____

_____

_____

8. What access do you have to young people?

_____

_____

_____

9. What do you feel is your level of understanding of the minds of youth today?

_____

_____

_____

10. What access do you think young people have inside and around the Democratic National Convention?

_____

_____

_____

Final Interviewee Comments:

_____

_____

_____

Student Research Fellow's Notes:

_____

_____

_____

Appendix H

South Bay Project
Summer Research Project Survey
(Hip-Hop Group)

Background
Name:
School Attended:
Year in School:
Age:
Ethnicity:

Hip-hop Culture and Education
How many hip-hop CDs do you own? (Circle the best response)

Less than 5   5–10   10–15   15–20   more than 20

How many hours a week do you spend listening to hip-hop on the radio and watching videos on TV?

Less than 1   1–2   3–5   5–10   more than 10

What influence does hip-hop music and culture have on teens in the following areas (1= no influence; 5 = extreme influence)?

Teens choice of clothing:

| 1 | 2 | 3 | 4 | 5 |
| No influence | | | | Extreme influence |

Teens' Speech (choice of language):

| 1 | 2 | 3 | 4 | 5 |
| No influence | | | | Extreme influence |

Teens' attitude toward authority figures:

1	2	3	4	5
No influence				Extreme influence

Teen's attitudes toward America:

1	2	3	4	5
No influence				Extreme influence

Overall, does hip-hop have a positive or negative impact on young people? Explain.

Why, in your opinion, is hip-hop music so widely listened to by young people?

How do your teachers feel about hip-hop music?

Would you like to see hip-hop included in what is taught in school? Explain.

Appendix I

Hip-Hop Project
Interview Protocols for Students and Teachers

Questions for Students:
1. How many hip-hop CDs do you own?
2. How many hours a week do you spend listening to hip-hop music on the radio and MTV?
3. What impact, if any, does hip-hop music have on the way you dress? The language you use?
4. Who is your favorite hip-hop artist? What is it that you admire about this artist?
5. Why do you feel that hip-hop music is so popular with young people today?
6. Do you feel that hip-hop music helps address the experiences of being young in a big city? If so, explain.
7. What impact, if any, does hip-hop music have on the way you view the world?
8. What attention, if any, do the teachers at your school give to hip-hop music? How do you think your teachers feel about hip-hop music? Why?
9. Do you feel that hip-hop music, or the issues discussed in hip-hop music, should be a part of the school curriculum? Why?
10. Would you like to see hip-hop music, film, or other elements of youth culture as part of the school curriculum? If so, how should it be included?
11. If you had the power, how would you change the high school curriculum? Why?

Questions for Teachers
1. Where do you teach? How many years have you taught? What subject(s) do you teach?
2. What is your opinion on utilizing the cultural perspectives of students in your curriculum?

3. In your opinion, how well do the curricula at your school address the cultural perspectives of the students at your school? Do you have any examples?

4. What experience have you had with hip-hop music?

5. What influence do you believe that hip-hop music has on urban America? On the students you teach? Why?

6. How do you define culture? According to your definition, does hip-hop constitute a culture? Why or why not?

Appendix J

Popular Culture Sourcebook

Agee on Film
Originally published by New York's Grosset and Dunlap in 1969, James Agee's *Agee on Film* is a classic in film theory and criticism.

AllHipHop.com (www.allhiphop.com)
Proclaimed as the most dangerous site on the Internet, this site combines the news of the latest developments in the industry with a social action and political bent. The site includes editorials, interviews, coverage of protests, debates, advertisements for books, and critical commentary from the architects of the culture showing that there is much more to hip-hop culture than top-40 hits.

Amazon.com (www.amazon.com)
Amazon.com used to boast itself as the world's largest bookstore. Now it's simply an internet market. Through Amazon, users can order books, CDs, DVDs, electronic equipment, apparel, auto parts, and much more and have these items shipped directly to their homes, thereby precluding the need for physical stores. Amazon.com is a prototype of e-commerce. It is also an excellent source for access to the sum creative output of popular culture along with the latest commentary and gadgetry associated with popular media.

American Film Institute (AFI) Desk Reference (www.afi.com)
The AFI desk reference provides a comprehensive summary of the first century of American cinema including biographical information on famous actors, background and commentary on classic films, and an introduction to the basic elements of film production. The AFI is probably most well known for their list of the top-100 American films of the last 100 years. It is also possible to get the list from the web site without purchasing the desk reference.

Cosmo Girl Magazine (www.cosmogirl.com)
Cosmo Girl is a fashion magazine targeting teen girls that features articles on movie stars, fitness, dating, and the latest happenings in

the teen world. In addition, *Cosmo Girl* contains feature stories that discuss the hardships and triumphs associated with being a teen girl. And, oh yeah, it contains its share of advertisements that promote the latest in teen fashion.

Cyber Film School (www.cyberfilmschool.com)
This site aims to offer a set of resources for self-training filmmakers and other fans of cinema. It features the Movie School Encyclopedia as well as articles, demonstrations, movie-making advice, and links to other film-related cites.

E! Online (www.eonline.com)
E! Online features the latest in movie news including reviews and features. The site provides a good snapshot of the latest films in the industry.

Ellie Girl
With departments that include global girl, shop girl, pretty girl, fan girl, and total girl, *Ellie Girl* is another in a long line of style and fashion magazines that work to dictate and co-opt a constantly emerging teen culture (see also *Seventeen*, *Teen Vogue*, and *YM*). As with the others, pay special attention to the advertisements that reveal volumes about how teen culture is marketed by major corporations at the same time that it exists in opposition to mainstream values.

Entertainment Weekly (www.ew.com)
Entertainment Weekly is probably the best source for up-to-date information across the range of popular media including film, television, music, and books. Each edition will feature top-grossing movies, highest-rated television shows, best-selling music, and best-selling books. Issues also feature critical commentary as well as previews of coming attractions. If you had to browse one magazine to learn what was hot at the moment, *Entertainment Weekly* would be my recommendation.

ESPN, The Magazine (www.espn.com)
ESPN The Magazine is an all access pass to the world of American professional sports. The magazine contains the wealth of information coupled with the humor and wit that viewers have come to

expect from the cable television station of the same name. Besides being a great magazine, *ESPN* features the best in sports writing. In fact, the magazine's popular writing is worthwhile for all students of writing, even non-sports fans.

Film.com (www.filmcom)
This site features movie reviews, news, and interviews: A great (and free) way to access the latest in blockbuster films.

The Film Encyclopedia, 4th Edition
The Film Encyclopedia is a handy A–Z reference with entries covering directors, actors, films, and genres that have defined the movie industry for a century. The book is also a source of information about the terminology and technology of a constantly evolving medium. Originally written by Ephraim Katz, the 4th Edition of *The Film Encyclopedia* is published by Harper Resource.

Filmmaker.com (www.filmmaker.com)
This is a great site for independent filmmakers. The site features articles, links, and downloads. It also offers a forum for filmmakers to exchange information with one another about making and distributing films.

Filmmaker Magazine
Filmmaker Magazine is targeted toward independent filmmakers and film fans. The magazine features articles on upcoming independent films, conversations with independent filmmakers, and information about the newest and latest technology in filmmaking. The magazine also advertises products for filmmakers and provides classifieds for industry professionals to solicit screenplays, actors, and movie crew personnel.

The Filmmaker's Handbook
The handbook is a succinct introductory guide to the process of filmmaking for teachers and students more interested in the production aspects of filmmaking as opposed to literary and textual analysis. The book, however, does provide rich language for use in film criticism that includes shots, composition, lighting, editing, and sequencing to name a few. The newly updated edition contains ample resources on digital filmmaking for the budding amateur filmmakers in class. *The Filmmaker's Handbook* is published by Plume.

Film Theory and Criticism: Introductory Readings, 5th Edition
This text, edited by Leo Braudy and Marshall Cohen and published by Oxford Press, is another excellent source of classic and contemporary film theory and criticism for teachers and students of film studies.

Game Now
Game Now contains the best codes, tips, and tricks for all of the latest video games. The magazine also features previews of the newest games and game systems and conversations with leading designers and artists. Be sure that there is a heavy dose of advertisements for the latest in games and game systems. There is also a section for subscriber submissions on favorite tricks and strategies for the most popular games. *Game Now* is arguably the most dog-eared magazine in the bookstore which says something about young people and their literacy habits. For other magazines on video games, see also *X Box Magazine, PC Gamer, Electronic Gaming Monthly* (www.egmag.com), and *Play Station Magazine* (www.playstation magazine.com) to name a few.

GL (Girls Life) Magazine (www.girlslife.com)
How to get beautiful, what foods to eat, self-esteem boosters for your shape and size, ice breakers for first dates, and how to find out if your guy is right for you. *GL* also features the latest and hottest in movies, music CDs, and concert tours in addition to party ideas and horoscopes.

Google.com (www.google.com)
One of the more powerful search engines on the web. A search engine responds to queries that users have about web content related to particular topics of interest. Users simply type in a word, phrase, or question and Google will provide the most commonly visited sites. The search engine is so common that many techies will use "google" as a verb synonym for a web search. Other search engines include Ask Jeeves (www.askjeeves. com), Excite (www.excite.com), and www.about.com.

HCI (Hot Compact and Imports) Magazine (www.hcimagazine.com)
HCI is one among a growing number of the "fast and furious" car magazines. One read through this magazine will convince you of the technical sophistication required of central or peripheral participants in the import car scene. The articles are a clever juxtaposition of

esoteric "how-to" car talk and hipster language symbolizing the marriage of car racing and youth spirit that have created this cultural phenomenon.

History of Cinema for Beginners

Part of the Writers and Readers comic book series of "for beginners" texts, the *History of Cinema for Beginners* is an accessible, yet informative text that covers the first century of cinema from a global perspective introducing key players, films, and advances in filmmaking technology. This is an excellent source for teachers and students interested in the history and evolution of the film industry.

Import Racer Magazine

Yet another teen zine with fast tricked-out cars. Plenty of great pictures, advertisements for everything you could ever want for your street racer, not to mention a heavy dose of import racing terminology.

Import Tuner Magazine (www.importtuner.com)

Seen *Fast and Furious*? *2Fast, 2Furious*? Maybe if you've only seen the commercials on television, or advertisements on billboards, you'll have an idea of how the import car racing scene is impacting youth popular culture. This particular magazine features plenty of photographs of fast and furious cars along with plenty of advertisements for any car accessory one can imagine. Don't be surprised to see young women and men who are too young to drive salivating over cars they cannot afford in the first place. Oh, did I mention the video game?

indieWIRE.com (www.indiewire.com)

This online web site for independent filmmakers includes movie reviews, interviews with independent professionals, and complete coverage of the major film festivals that screen independent films.

Interview Magazine

Interview magazine features intimate conversations with the leading players in Hollywood for those interested in the private lives and motivations of the industry's elite.

Introduction to Film Studies (www.routledge.com)

This comprehensive text covers the history and technology of film as well as various approaches to studying film texts such as the film form as narrative, the film spectator, and genre, star, and auteur theories. It also provides insight on how to study and write about documentaries and animation. This introductory text presents case studies as examples of the various approaches it explicates. Intended as a primer for the beginning student of film, the book provides an excellent vocabulary to discuss and write about this genre. *Introduction to Film Studies* is published by Routledge.

Leonard Maltin's 2003 Movie & Video Guide
A leader in the movie review business provides his encyclopedia of film reviews, which includes 19,000 entries. Maltin's guide is a good source for finding pertinent information and succinct commentary on popular films, the classics, as well as less known films that have been critically acclaimed. The book is another must-have for the film library of the teacher or student interested in the study of film. The paperbacks are extremely affordable. *Leonard Maltin's 2003 Movie & Video Guide* is published by Plume.

Lyrics.com (www.lyrics.com)
This is a great site for teachers who want to teach popular music selections and are interested in acquiring lyrics. Once on the site, it is possible to search for lyrics by artists. Most of the popular artists are available through this site.

Mac World (www.macworld.com)
This is the self-proclaimed magazine of choice for Apple Macintosh users. The magazine contains a wealth of information for consumers and enthusiasts of Macintosh products from the beginners to experts. There are plenty of advertisements, previews, reviews and useful information, particularly for those interested in multimedia consumption and production, whether music, photography, digital filmmaking, or web logs (blogs). See also *Mac Addict*, another magazine for Macintosh users.

Modified Magazine (www.modified.com)
You guessed it! Another magazine featuring fast import cars. In addition to technical articles, feature cars, and scores of advertisements for car racing equipment and accessories, *Modified* provides coverage of drivers and events in import car racing and drifting along with photographs and commentary of the shows that reveal the newest and slickest in import car technology.

Movie Maker Magazine (www.moviemaker.com)
This quarterly publication is targeted toward the independent film-maker. *Movie Maker* features interviews with leading independent directors, previews of upcoming indie films, analyses of trends in technology and film production as well as a current calendar of indie film culture. The advertisements for contests, film schools, and equipment also provide a sampling of the opportunities available and a snapshot of the latest in digital film technology. Many of the contests and advertisements appeal directly to adolescents, who are increasingly becoming involved in amateur filmmaking due to the decreasing costs associated with such an enterprise.

MTV.com (www.mtv.com)
This is the official web site for MTV (Music Television), one of the most widely accessed popular cultural sites. The cable television station features music videos, game shows, concert footage, and reality television shows. The web site features a search engine for information on the latest bands, television schedules for MTV and MTV2, links to all of the station's reality shows, links to videos, MTV news, and even shopping.

The Off-Hollywood Film Guide
This book is a great resource for lovers of independent and foreign films. *The Off-Hollywood Film Guide* features production and casting information and plot synopses for those "essential" independent and foreign films that are difficult to access through mainstream channels. If you're having difficulty locating these films at the local video store, try www.netflixx.com.

Oscar.com (www.oscar.com)
This is the official web site of the Academy Awards. The site includes a complete database of past award winners and is a great resource for teachers interested in including the study of film and cinema in their literacy classrooms.

PC Magazine (www.pcmag.com)
This magazine contains all of the newest and latest in hardware, software, and gadgetry for the PC (Personal computer) enthusiasts and those just looking to upgrade their system. *PC Magazine* contains a combination of advertisements, product previews, reviews, and forecasts for future trends in a digital revolution that includes

cameras, phonecams (cell phones with built in digital cameras), and handheld computing devices. The magazine includes "how-to" sections for beginners. For other PC magazines see *Maximum PC, PC Plus*, and *PC World*.

The Pocket Essential Blaxpoitation Films (www.pocketessentials. com)
This is a short but handy reference text that covers a progressive era in African American filmmaking. It features a wonderful introductory essay as well as a review of essential films produced during this era. In addition to the Blaxpoitation text, Pocket Essentials features a host of other texts on noteworthy topics and personalities of film. For more information, check the pocket essentials web site.

Rap Lyrics Search.com (www.raplyricssearch.com)
This site provides easy access to the lyrics of all of the major stars in the hip-hop industry. This is a great resource for teachers who want to include hip-hop selections in their classroom units.

Roger Ebert's Movie Yearbook 2003
Ebert's book features 600+ reviews of movies that debuted from January 1, 2000 through July 2002 and is an excellent resource for contemporary popular movies that premiered during this period. It is also a superb example of popular film review from one of the most respected in the business. This book is published by Andrews McMeel Publishing.

Rolling Stone Magazine (www.rollingstone.com)
Rolling Stone is undoubtedly the oldest and most popular of rock and roll magazines with a scope that includes multiple genres of music and popular culture. Each issue includes interviews and editorials in addition to music, film, and book reviews. More than some of the other popular magazines, *Rolling Stone* features political commentary written from a young, progressive point of view. It is not uncommon to see major political figures discussing youth issues with magazine reporters or to find the latest world crises examined from an untraditional lens.

The Rough Guide to Hip-Hop (www.roughguides.com)
The Rough Guide to Hip-Hop is an excellent historical source of hip-hop music and culture that can fit into your pocket. More than any other text, the *Rough Guide* provides extensive biographies of all of

the names that have created hip-hop culture along with critical commentaries of their best and worst work. Texts like the *Rough Guide* are a nice supplement to the popular magazines that feature the now of hip-hop culture and provide a firm grounding in the foundations and evolution of the culture. The *Rough Guide* will also make an excellent resource for student aficionados assembling hip-hop collections. There are also other *Rough Guides* such as: The *Rough Guide to Rock*, the *Rough Guide to the Internet*, and the *Rough Guide to House Music*.

scr(i)pt Magazine

For teachers and students that are so inclined, *scr(i)pt* provides commentary from screenwriters on their craft and an analysis of upcoming attractions from the point of view of screenwriters and directors. *scr(i)pt* is also a source of the latest information about upcoming film festivals, screenwriting contests, and other opportunities for novices to submit their work to industry professionals. It also provides a listing of workshops, programs, and resources available for novices who wish to improve their craft.

Seventeen Magazine (www.seventeen.com)

Along with *YM*, this is the primary magazine targeted toward adolescent girls. It features departments that include: fashion, beauty, health, love, real life, stars, and life guide. *Seventeen* provides an interesting juxtaposition of enabling narratives of young women and the production of consumers via its advertising campaigns for the latest in fashion and style.

Sg (Surf, Snow, Skate Girl) Magazine (www.sgmag.com)

Sg Magazine targets young women that are into the surfing, skateboarding, and snowboarding scene. The magazine articles feature coverage of competitive events such as the Winter X games, the best places to surf, skate, and snowboard, and, of course, the latest fashion and gear to ensure that enthusiasts stay safe and look good while practicing their craft.

Skateboarder Magazine (www.skateboardermag.com)

Awesome photographs of amateurs and professionals landing cool tricks, such as rail crushers, 180 nosegrinds, and flip tricks. Skateboarder also features reviews of skateboarding videos; advertisements for the shoes, shirts, glasses, hats, boards, and other sundry accessories that define the culture; competition coverage; biographical information on the hottest skaters; the best places to skate; and, of course, the latest, craziest tricks.

SLAM Magazine (www.slamonline.com)
Hoops meets hip-hop in this sports and culture fan magazine. *Slam* provides a combination of stories of NBA teams and players and presentation of professional basketball players as representatives of youth culture rather than being substantively about the discourse of sports per se. Check out the advertisements for the shoes and fashion that are the hallmarks of youth popular culture.

The Source Magazine
Along with *Vibe*, *The Source* is a premier magazine of hip-hop music and culture. The monthly magazine is noted for its crisp and no-nonsense interviews and reviews of artists and their music. Probably a bit more politicized and edgier than *Vibe*, *The Source* is a mainstream publication that makes an effort to promote and represent the underground and marginalized element within the culture. In this way, it is similar to what *Spin* does for the Rock industry. The advertisements in *The Source* are a panoptic of the contemporary fashion and tastes of the hip-hop culture, revealing it to be about more than just the music.

Sporting News Sports Guides (www.sportingnews.com)
In addition to their regularly released periodical of sports writing, *Sporting News* offers a host of pre-season guides for football (college and professional), basketball (college and professional), baseball, and hockey. These guides contain analyses, predictions, rosters, and schedules for all of the teams and players. They are a great resource to use when watching major college or professional sports.

Sports Illustrated Magazine (www.cnnsi.com)
Straight sports, no chaser. *Sports Illustrated* is not generally the contemporary choice of young America with other options such as *Slam* out there, but it is the oldest and most noted of sports magazines. No offense to the magazine, but for the latest statistics, it is probably easiest to go to the ESPN web site or just watch Sports Center on ESPN. On the other hand, *Sports Illustrated for Kids* and *Sports Illustrated for Women* are excellent magazines that feature content not normally available through other popular media.

Spin Magazine (www.spin.com)

Spin is best known for its coverage of the progressive or alternative music scene. In addition to mainstream and best-selling artists, *Spin* attempts to cover groups and artists on the fringe of the music industry that are countercultural, political, offensive, that feature a unique and esoteric sound, or even groups and artists that are trying to produce socially conscious music. Count on *Spin* to give serious coverage of that important band that is just off the popular radar screen. As with *Rolling Stone, Spin* provides in-depth investigative reporting on a slew of issues, from politics to pop culture. Reviews, essays, profiles, and interviews make up a package of pure rock energy with an alternative all "spun" with that progressive edge.

Street and Smiths Sports Guides

Just like *Sporting News, Street and Smith's* puts out pre-season guides for NCAA Basketball, NCAA Football, the NFL, the NHL, the NBA, and Major League Baseball. These guides provide rosters, statistics, and analyses of the strengths and weaknesses of each team along with predictions for All-Star selections and season outcomes. Having a *Street and Smith* guide is like having a program for every team. Look for these guides to hit shelves 4–6 weeks before the start of the season.

Surfer Magazine (www.surfermag.com)

Surfer is a magazine created for the surfing enthusiast or those that long to be. The magazine features elite surfers and the fashion, gear, and lingo that comprise everyday surfer culture.

Surfing Magazine (www.surfingthemag.com)

Surfing magazine also targets the surfing aficionado and is replete with coverage of the top events, information on the best places to catch a wave, advice on tricks of the trade, and a heavy dose of articles and advertisements pertaining to boards and other gear. As with many other magazines and websites, the articles in *Surfing* provide a window into the latest innovations in surfer language and culture.

Teen Magazine (www.teen.com)

This magazine is replete with pin-ups and interviews of the latest teen idols in music, film, and television. The magazine also contains a heavy dose of fashion, beauty, and health tips. Advertisements for the latest gear, videogames, and game systems can also be found in *Teen*. Further, the magazine features articles on romance and the latest scoops on the hottest teens in the biz. It's another good magazine to learn about the stars of right now in teen popular culture.

Teen People (www.teenpeople.com)

Teen People is probably the most widely read entertainment magazine targeted specifically toward teens. Like its adult counterpart, *Teen People* features the latest of the on and off stage lives of the industry's giants. Unlike the adult counterpart, the magazine also features back to school fashion tips, dating advice, make-over tips, and pull-out posters.

Teen Vogue (www.teenvogue.com)

Along with *Seventeen*, *YM*, and *Ellie girl*, this is another fashion-oriented magazine targeted toward middle and high school girls. The magazine features an occasional article about young womanhood surrounded by 200 or so pages of the latest in teen fashion.

Time Out Film Guide

Time Out features over 14,000 films reviewed by its critics. The text is self-proclaimed as an encyclopedia for film buffs for valid and obvious reasons. Honestly, I could not locate a film with which I was familiar that was not covered in the book. *Time Out* is an excellent resource for teachers and students with an interest in film studies. Each review provides information for the director, screenwriter, editors, and key cast members. This volume also contains indices that allow readers to look up films by actors and directors. The *Time Out Film Guide* is published by Penguin.

Total Television

Total Television provides a comprehensive guide of television programming from the late 1940s through the end of the twentieth century. The selections include daytime and prime time series, specials, and prime time schedules for the networks over the years. *Total Television* also includes Emmy Award winners, Neilsen's top-rated programs, as well an index for quick searching. This book is a great resource for teachers interested in the history and culture of television. *Total Television* is written by Alex McNeil and published by Penguin.

TV Guide (www.tvguide.com)

TV Guide is still the most comprehensive source for answering the question of "what's on tonight?" In addition to the famous weekly lineups, *TV Guide* also features valuable commentary on contemporary television programming.

TV Guide Film and Video Companion

The *TV Guide Film and Video Companion* features fewer entries (3,500) than some of the other guides I have mentioned, but these entries contain more substantive information on the films listed including academy award nominations, complete cast listings, and plot synopses. The guide also contains an actor's index, a director's index, and a star rating index that allows a snapshot of the most highly acclaimed movies. The *TV Guide Film and Video Companion* is published by Friedman/Fairfax.

URB Magazine (www.clickurb.com)

On the postmodern, progressive edge of the "popular" along with rave DJs and underground clubs, sits *URB*, the self-proclaimed magazine of future music and culture. In *URB*, you'll find the latest in fashion and musings of club culture along with reviews of the latest in hip-hop, house, techno, trance, breakbeat, jungle, downtempo, and experimental music. *URB* also reaches beyond music and the club scene to cover topics ranging from hypermedia to Japanese Anime.

Variety.com (www.variety.com)

This is the official web site for the industry magazine *Variety*. It features industry news, box-office information, and reviews of recently released and upcoming movies.

The Vibe History of Hip-Hop

As of the publication of this book, *The Vibe History of Hip-Hop* is still the definitive encyclopedia of the culture. Filled with comprehensive historical information on the eras of hip-hop and their stars, a reading of this text will leave any novice grounded in the past and present of hip-hop, at least as it was experienced through mainstream America. Check out the *Rough Guide* for a better sense of the underground classics. Also, don't look to this text for the stars of the moment. A glance at the covers of *Vibe, The Source, Rap Pages,* or *Rolling Stone* will reveal who's hot.

Vibe Magazine (www.vibe.com)
Vibe is the self-proclaimed voice of urban culture and I would be hesitant to argue with that description. Quantitatively, it is definitely the best selling of hip-hop periodicals. The monthly magazine provides an accurate snapshot of the latest in mainstream hip-hop culture with its interviews, columns, and analyses of musical selections. *Vibe* illustrates hip-hop's expansive role in popular culture through its documentation of the relationship between hip-hop, professional sports, and Hollywood film. *Vibe* also plays a large role in documenting and marketing the present and future in hip-hop fashion.

Video Hound's DVD Guide Book 2
If you're into buying or renting DVDs, you'll understand the importance of this guide, which features previews and analyses of 5,000 films currently out on DVDs. The guide assesses the quality of the DVD transfer and delineates all of the additional features such as deleted scenes, documentaries, and critical commentary that make DVDs such essential resources for film aficionados. *Video Hound's DVD Guide Book 2* is published by the Gale Group.

Wired Magazine (www.wired.com)
From handheld computers, to phonecams, to the wireless internet, to the latest technological innovations in the increasingly interconnected world, this magazine targets a large audience ranging from cyberpunks to corporate CEOs offering the newest and best of the cyber-digital-IT revolution.

A Woman's View: How Hollywood Spoke to Women 1930–1960
This text, written by Jeanine Basinger and published by Knopf/Random House, provides an alternate look at the Hollywood Film industry and provides an entry point for feminist criticisms of Hollywood films.

Yahoo.com (www.yahoo.com)
Yahoo.com is the "Grand Central Station" of the Internet as the site features a host of services. Users can open and access e-mail accounts (*username@yahoo.com*), build personal web pages (via geocities), or join or create chat groups. *Yahoo.com* also features a search engine that is powered by google technology.

YM (www.ym.com)
YM is a magazine that targets an audience of adolescent girls and covers stories ranging from school survival and college access advice, to beauty and style tips, to teen Hollywood, to the science of understanding adolescent boys. Pay special attention to the advertisements that construct teen style even as they articulate teen culture.

Appendix K

Resources for Teachers Interested in Action Research

Action Research: Principles and Practice (Jean McNiff, 1988; published by Routledge): McNiff's book encourages teachers to use action research as a strategy for improving their classroom practice. Her book outlines the philosophies and processes of action research by examining actual action research projects. It is a great source for classroom teachers to learn about the possibilities of researching their own practice.

Critical Encounters in High School English: Teaching Literary Theory to Adolescents (Deborah Appleman, 2000; published by TC Press/NCTE): Appleman's book is a great example of how university researchers and classroom teachers can collaborate to research classroom practice. She and a teacher colleague worked together to examine the outcomes associated with teaching literary theories in a high school classroom.

Critical Theory and Educational Research (Edited by Peter McLaren and James M. Giarelli, 1995; published by State University of New York Press): McLaren and Giarelli's edited volume feature essays and studies that consider research that is informed by critical theory and geared toward social change. McLaren and Giarelli's book challenges popular notions that research should be objective and that researchers should be distanced and disinterested participants. Rather, the essays and studies featured in this text contend for research that is interested and engaged as they challenge the who, what, and why of the educational tradition. This is an excellent book for teachers interested in research for social and political change.

English Journal: The *English Journal* is a monthly publication of the National Council of Teachers of English that targets secondary English teachers and teacher educators. At 66,000, it has a larger national audience than most professional journals and is an excellent source of published action research projects. It is possible to order the English Journal by becoming a member of NCTE at www.ncte.org.

The Ethnographer's Toolkit (Edited by Jean J. Schensul and Margaret LeCompte, 1999; published by Altamira Press): The ethnographer's toolkit is a set of seven volumes designed for the novice ethnographer. Written in a highly accessible format, the volumes take the beginning ethnographer through a step-by-step approach that proceeds from designing a study to collecting data, to data analysis to write up. The seven volumes include: (1) *Designing and Conducting Ethnographic Research;* (2) *Essential Ethnographic Methods: Observations, Interviews, and Questionnaires;* (3) *Enhanced Ethnographic Methods: Audiovisual Techniques, Focused Group Interviews, and Elicitation Techniques;* (4) *Mapping Social Networks, Spacial Data, and Hidden Populations;* (5) *Analyzing and Interpreting Ethnographic Data;* (6) *Researcher Roles and Research Partnerships;* and (7) *Using Ethnographic Data: Interventions, Public Programming, and Public Policy.*

Handbook of Research on Teaching the English Language Arts (Edited by James Flood, Diane Lapp, James R. Squire, and Julie Jensen, 2003; published by Lawrence Earlbaum Associates): This comprehensive volume traces developments in educational research as it relates to the teaching of English language arts. Of particular importance to action researchers is a section on methods of research on English language arts teaching.

International Reading Association (www.reading.org): The International Reading Association is an organization dedicated to improving reading achievement at the K–12 level. IRA hosts an annual convention where teachers and university faculty come together to present their research on classroom practice. The IRA convention provides a forum for teacher-researchers to share their work with one another. IRA also publishes manuscripts that feature teacher research.

Introducing Anthropology: Written by Merryl Wyn Davis and illustrated by Piero, *Introducing Anthropology* is published by Totem Books, a major producer of introductory comic texts that rivals the "for beginners" series. At any rate, *Introducing Anthropology* is a well-written, well-illustrated text that will quickly orient the novice to the history of the discipline including the greatest practitioners as well as the major developments and debates that have shaped the discipline thus far.

Journal of Adolescent and Adult Literacy (JAAL): The *Journal of Adolescent and Adult Literacy* is a publication of the International Reading Association that features research related to literacy development among teens and adults. JAAL is an excellent source of ideas on action research projects as well a site to submit reports of action research to an international audience that includes teachers, teacher educators, and university researchers.

Local Knowledge: Further Essays in Interpretive Ethnography (Clifford Geertz, 2000; published by Basic Books): *Local Knowledge* provides a collection of essays about the role of an ethnographer and the nature of ethnography from one of the best to ever practice the craft. Another more well known text written by Geertz is *The Interpretation of Cultures*, which is also published by Basic Books.

Modern Language Association (MLA) Handbook for Writers of Research Papers, 5th Edition: About half of the educational journals and book publishers will want manuscripts submitted to them in MLA format. The format generally refers to the preparation of the manuscript and the style of citing sources. The MLA manual offers assistance with both format and style and includes sections that cover in text citations, works cited sections, and sample pages of a manuscript prepared in MLA style. The manual is not only important for teachers but also for students who are developing and hopefully distributing their own action research projects.

National Council of Teachers of English (www.ncte.org): NCTE is the major national professional organization for teachers of English/ Language Arts. Every year, NCTE hosts an annual convention where teachers from across the country come to present their action research projects. NCTE also publishes numerous teacher research studies. From their web site, it is possible to access their catalog of past and present publications. In addition to the national organization, NCTE also has an affiliate in every state that also holds annual meetings and publishes state-wide newsletters and journals. All state affiliates are linked to the national web site.

National Writing Project (www.writingproject.org): The National Writing Project (NWP) is a national organization devoted to improving the teaching of writing at the K–12 level. The NWP's local affiliates usually host summer institutes for practicing teachers that are excellent sites for professional development and for learning how to develop classroom research projects that assess and document innovative writing instruction. For more information on local sites, consult the web site.

Publication Manual of the American Psychological Association (APA), 5th Edition: The other half of journals and book publishers will expect submitted manuscripts in the APA format. The 5th edition is a great resource for researchers and for teachers who are encouraging their students to become action researchers. The manual is quite thorough and is helpful for citation and for the formatting of manuscripts for publication. The 5th edition also features added sections for the documentation of Internet sources.

Qualitative Research and Case Study Applications in Education (Sharan B. Merriam, 1998; published by Jossey-Bass): Merriam's book takes the reader through a survey of qualitative research in education including descriptions of various qualitative methods that have been used in educational contexts and a step-by-step guide through the qualitative research process from design to writing reports.

Reinventing Anthropology (Edited by Dell Hymes, 1999; published by University of Michigan Press): Hymes and his colleagues call for an anthropology that is more progressive, political, and seeking liberatory ends rather than materialistic ones. Hymes' critical anthropology is ideal for teachers interested in using anthropological research for educational and social change.

Voices from the Middle: *Voices From the Middle* is a monthly publication of the National Council of Teachers of English that targets middle school teachers of English Language Arts. This is a good site to read about action research projects conducted by other teachers or to submit action research studies for others to read.

You Gotta BE the Book: Teaching Engaged and Reflective Reading With Adolescents (Jeffrey Wilhelm, 1997; published by TC Press/NCTE): Wilhelm provides a superior example of how teachers can design and carry out action research projects in their own classrooms.

Index

About the Author

Ernest Morrell is an assistant professor of teacher education at Michigan State University. For more than a decade he has worked with adolescents, drawing upon their involvement with popular culture to promote academic literacy development. Morrell is the author of one other book currently in press entitled *Becoming Critical Researchers: Literacy and Empowerment for Urban Youth.*